BIGFOOT:

ORIGINS

A Graphic Novel

BIGFOOT: ORIGINS

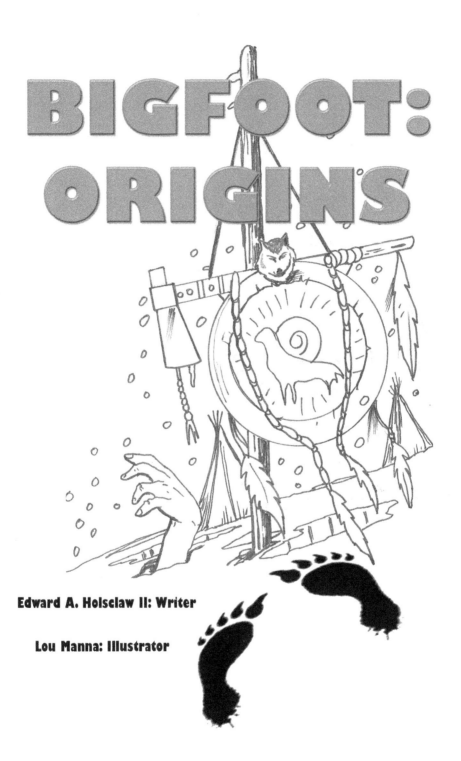

Edward A. Holsclaw II: Writer

Lou Manna: Illustrator

BIGFOOT: ORIGINS
A Graphic Novel

COPYRIGHT © 2023 BY EDWARD A. HOLSCLAW II
Paperback ISBN: 978-1-63073-446-6
Hard Cover ISBN: 978-1-63073-447-3
eBook ISBN: 978-1-63073-448-0

Illustrations by Lou Manna

PUBLISHED BY
FL Publishers

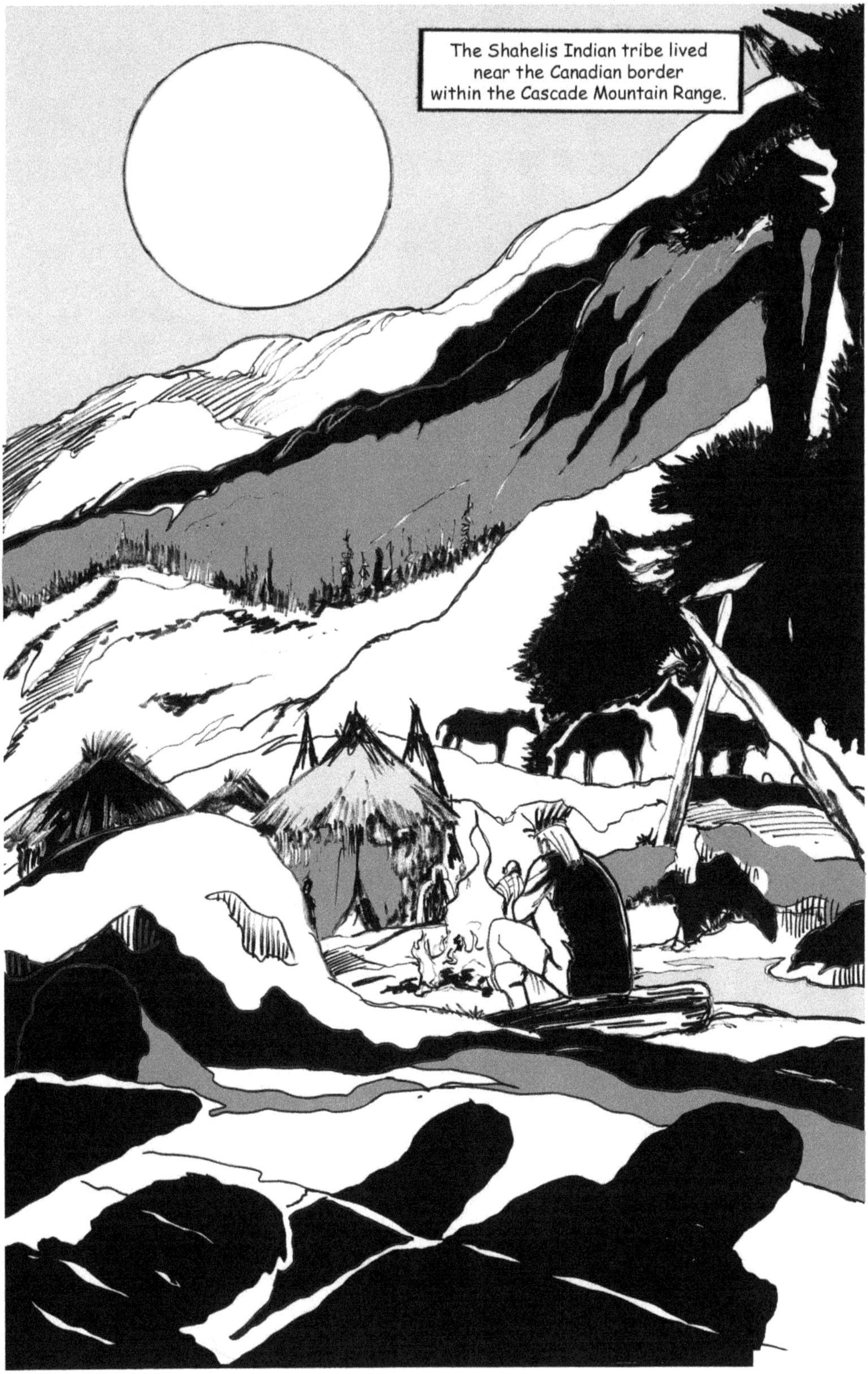
The Shahelis Indian tribe lived near the Canadian border within the Cascade Mountain Range.

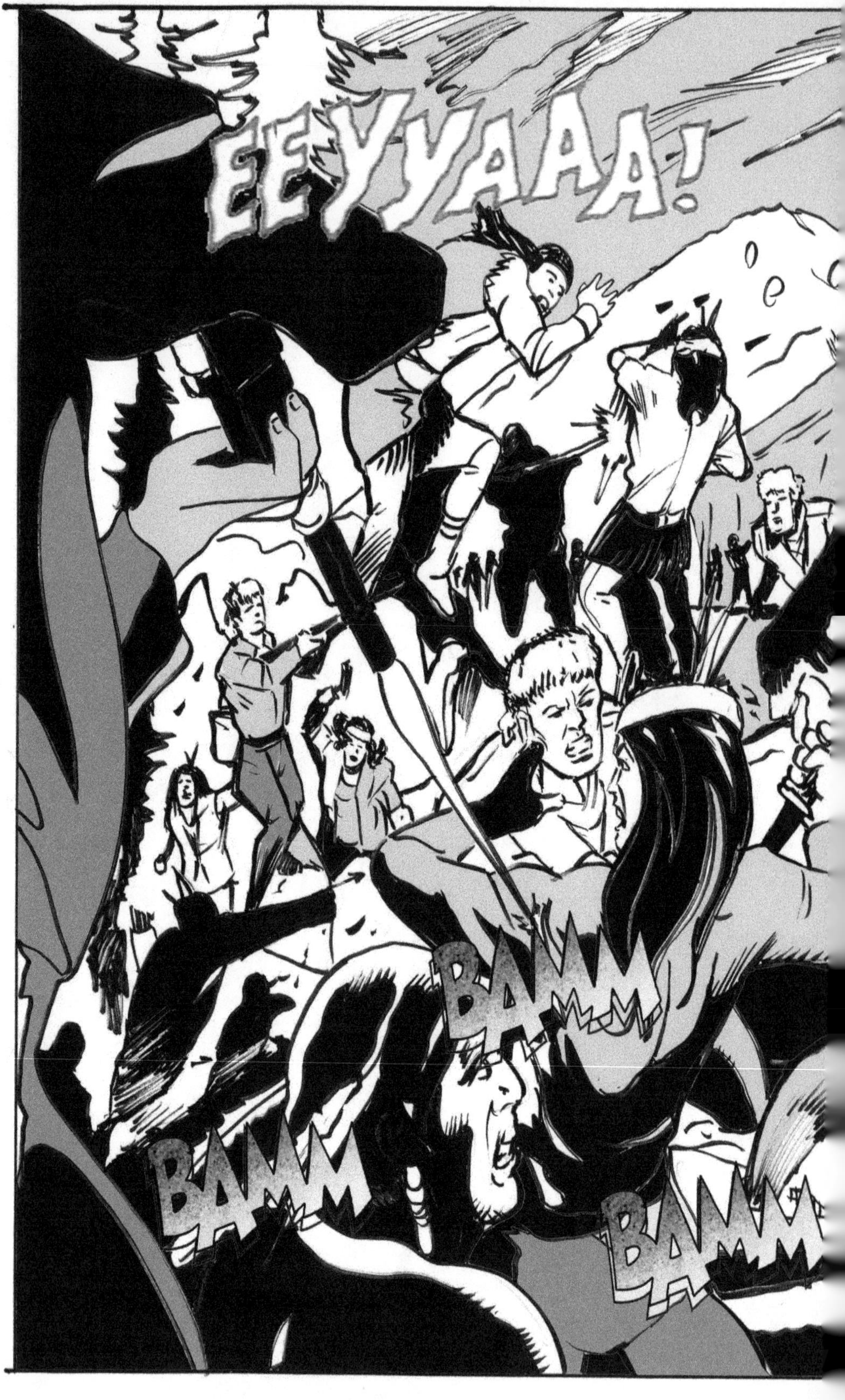
EEYYAAA!
BAMM
BAMM
BAMM

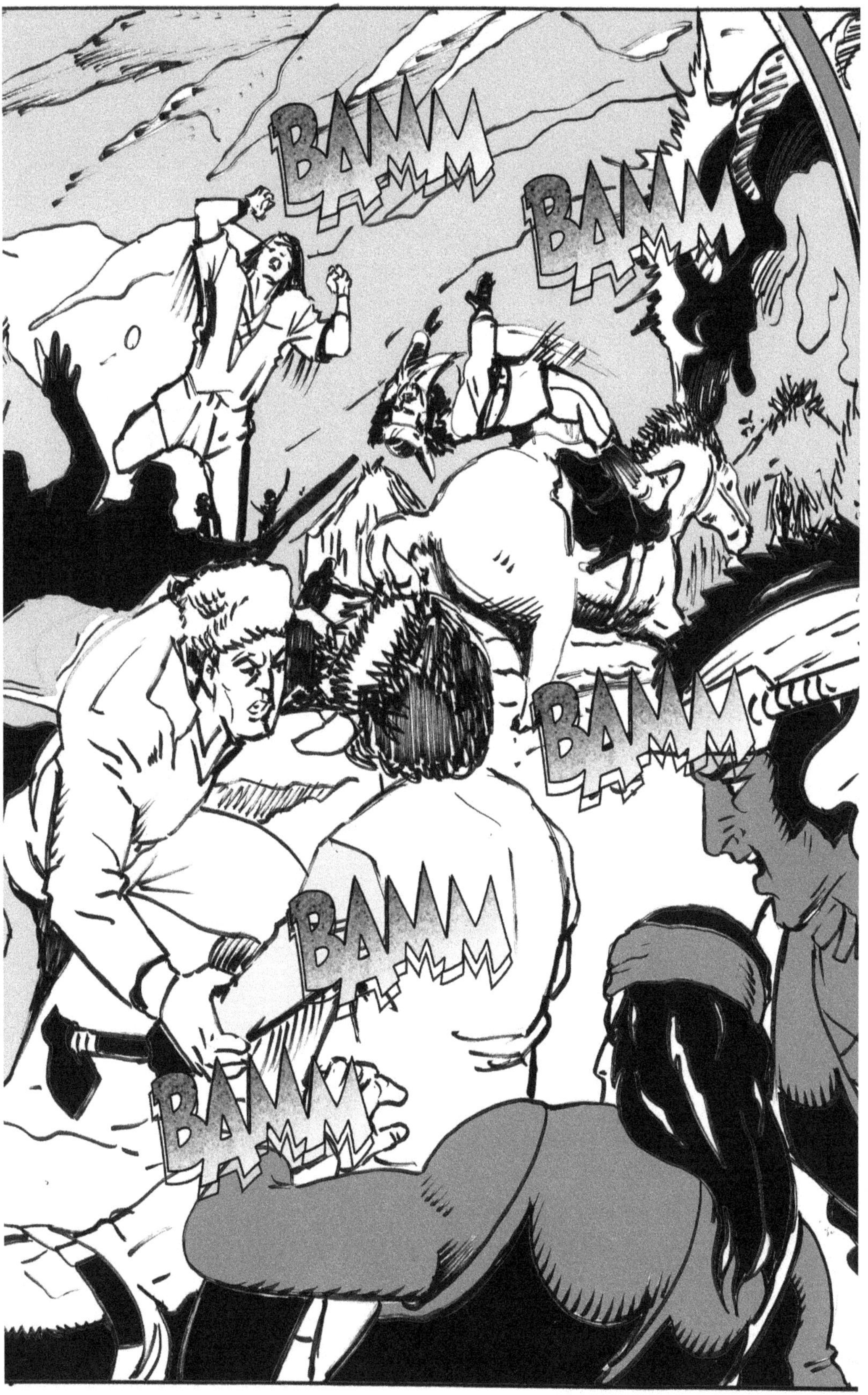
BAMM
BAMM
BAMM
BAMM
BAMM

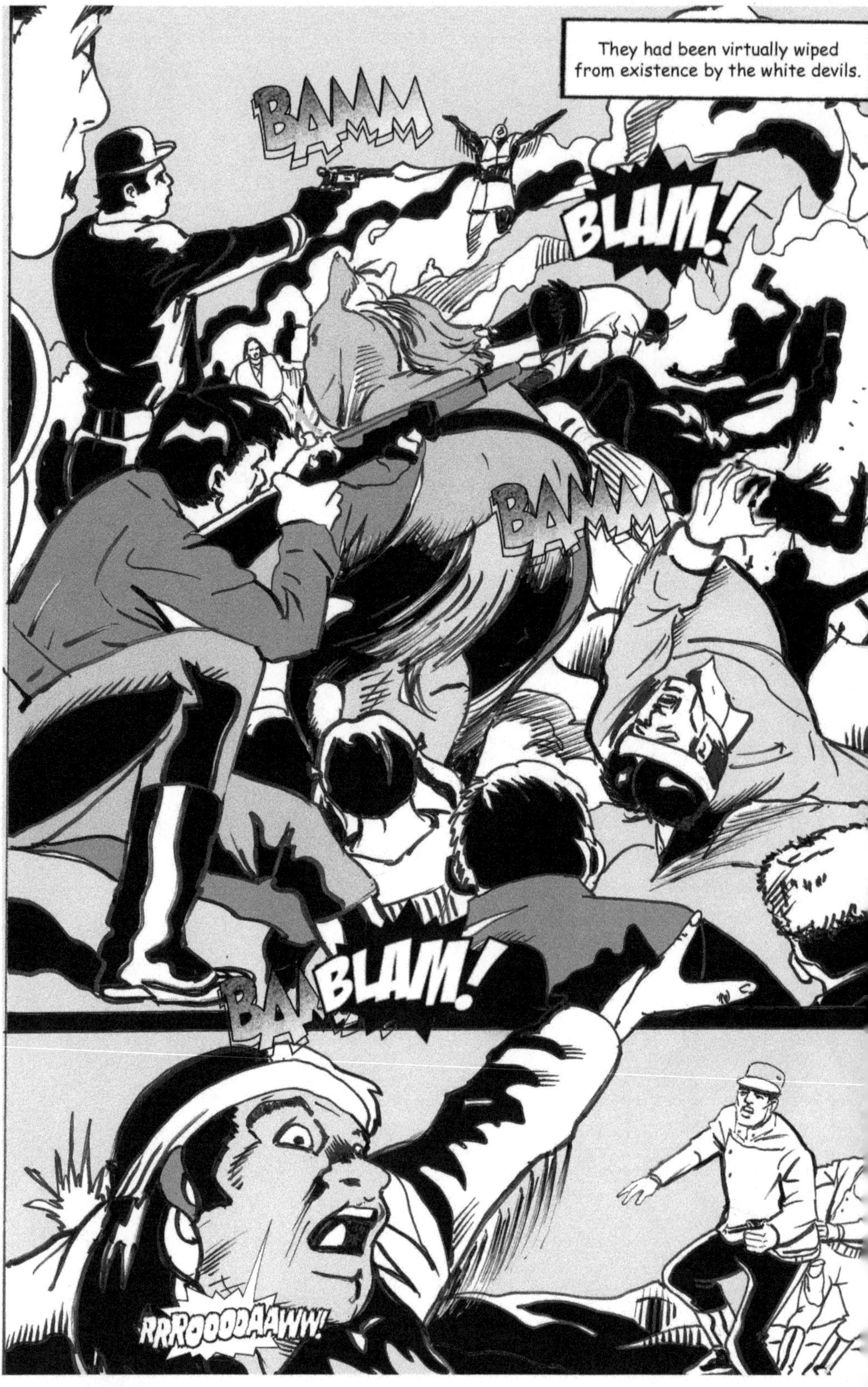
They had been virtually wiped from existence by the white devils.
BAMM
BLAM!
BAMM
BLAM!
RRROOOOAAWW!

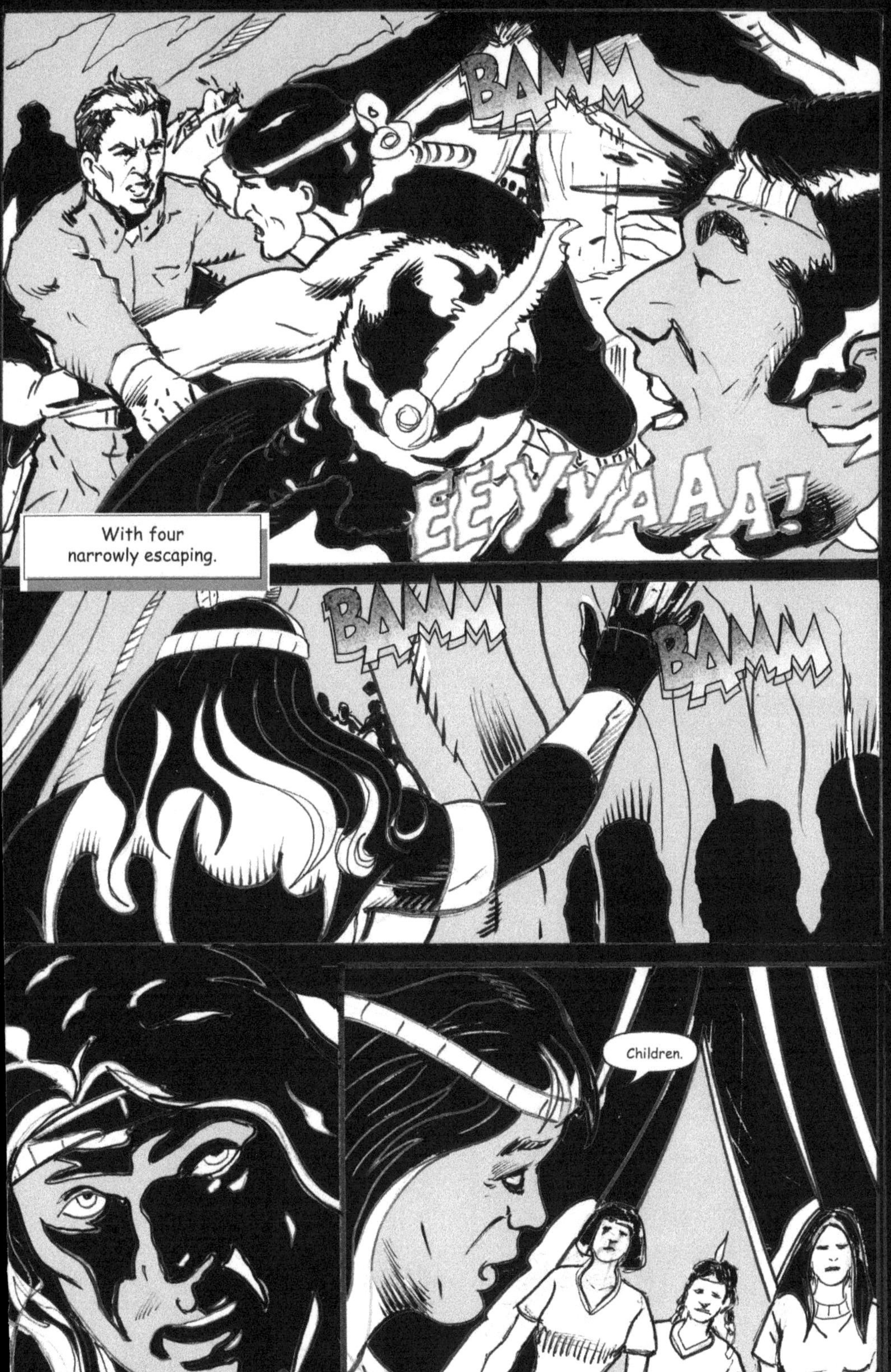
BAMM
EEYYAAA!
With four narrowly escaping.
BAMM
BAMM
Children.

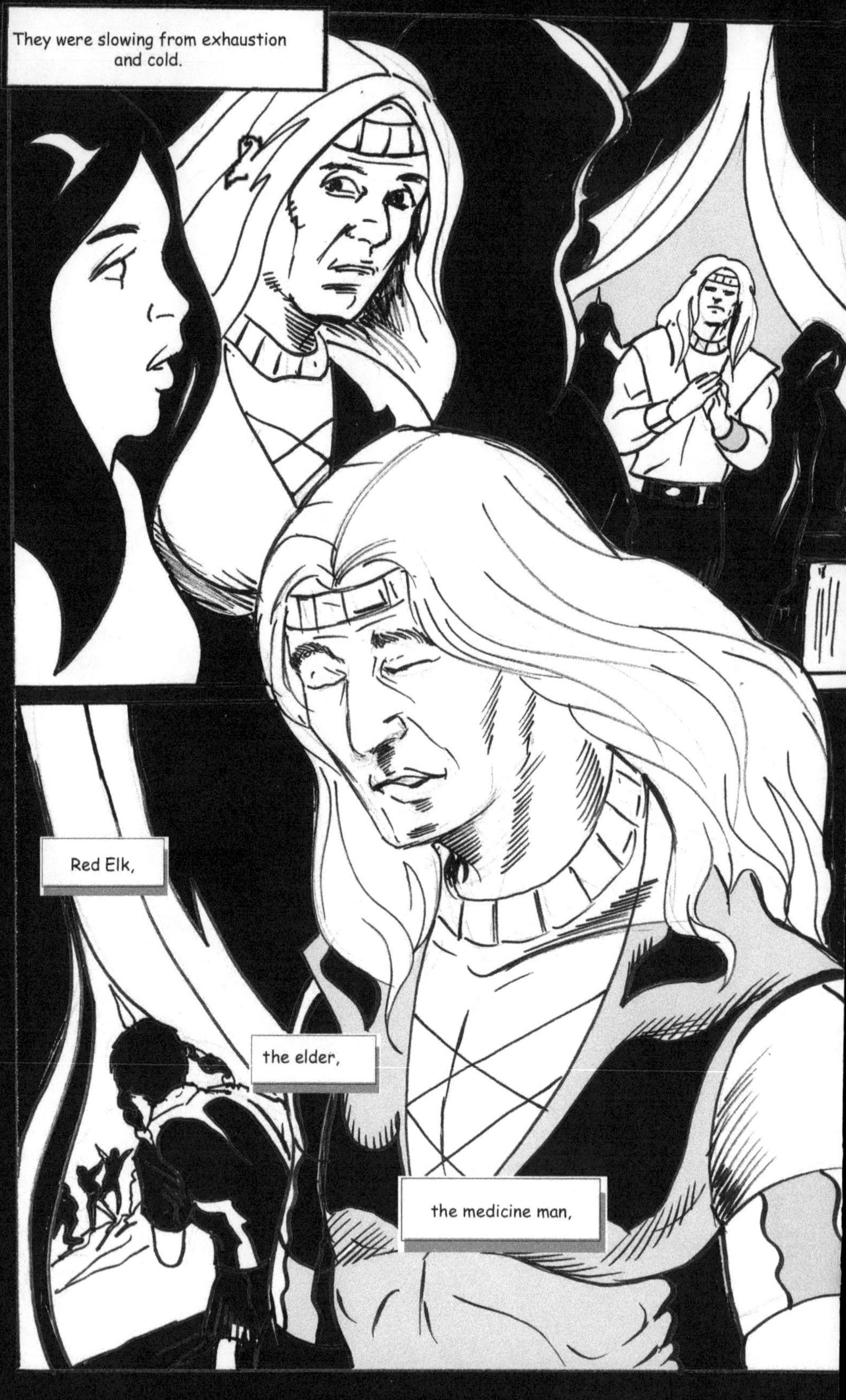
They were slowing from exhaustion and cold.
Red Elk,
the elder,
the medicine man,

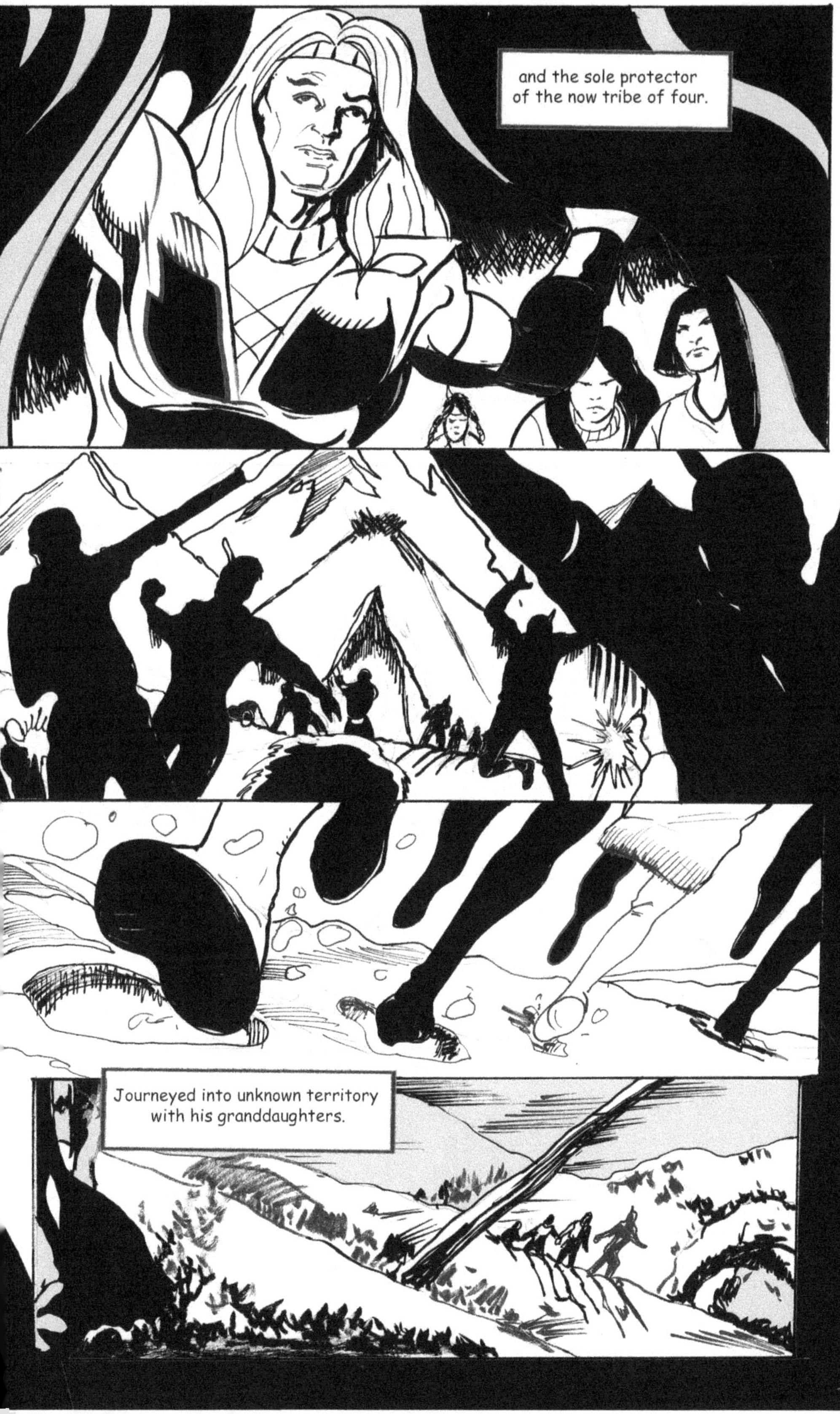
and the sole protector
of the now tribe of four.
Journeyed into unknown territory
with his granddaughters.

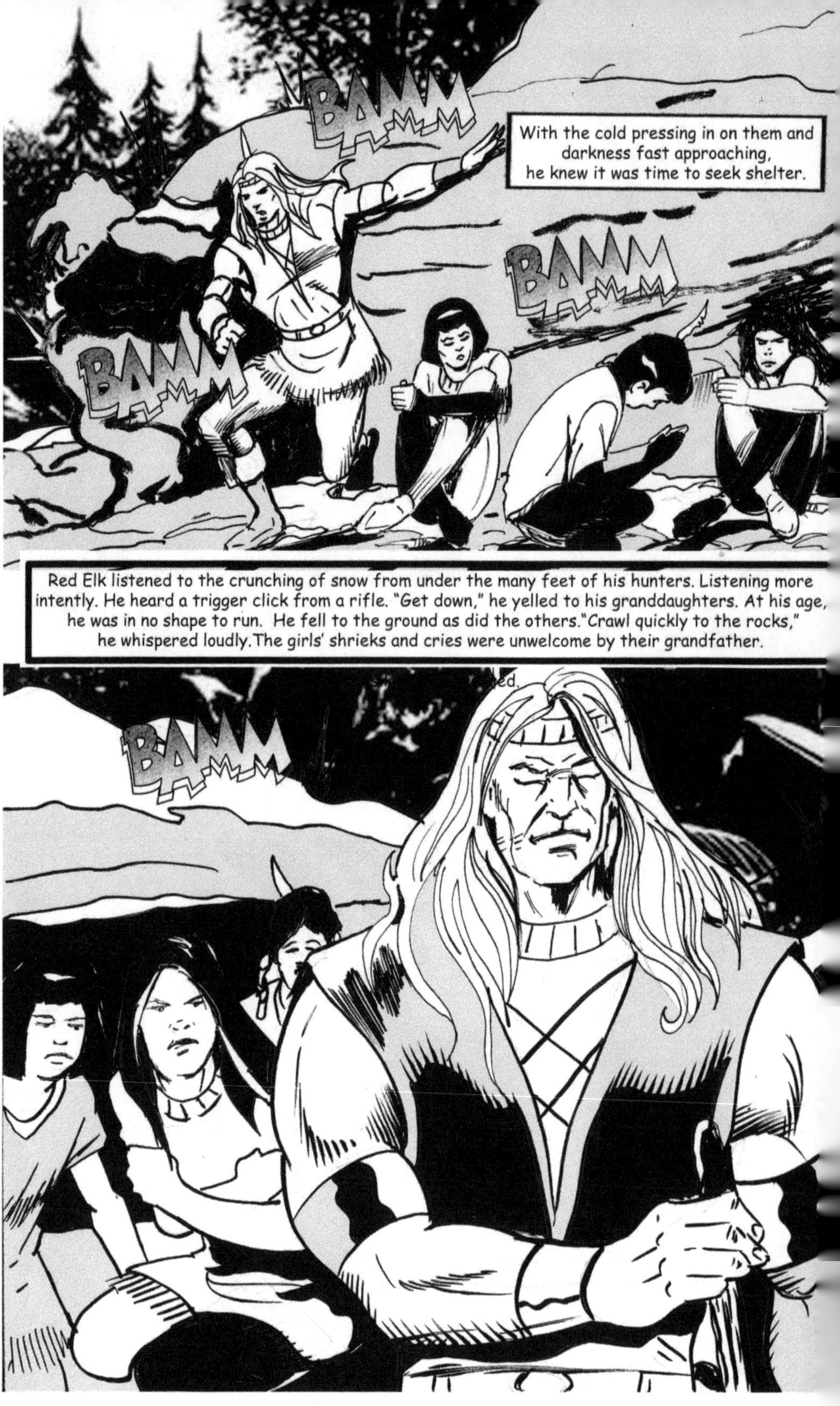
BAMM
With the cold pressing in on them and darkness fast approaching, he knew it was time to seek shelter.
BAMM
BAMM
Red Elk listened to the crunching of snow from under the many feet of his hunters. Listening more intently. He heard a trigger click from a rifle. "Get down," he yelled to his granddaughters. At his age, he was in no shape to run. He fell to the ground as did the others."Crawl quickly to the rocks," he whispered loudly.The girls' shrieks and cries were unwelcome by their grandfather.
BAMM

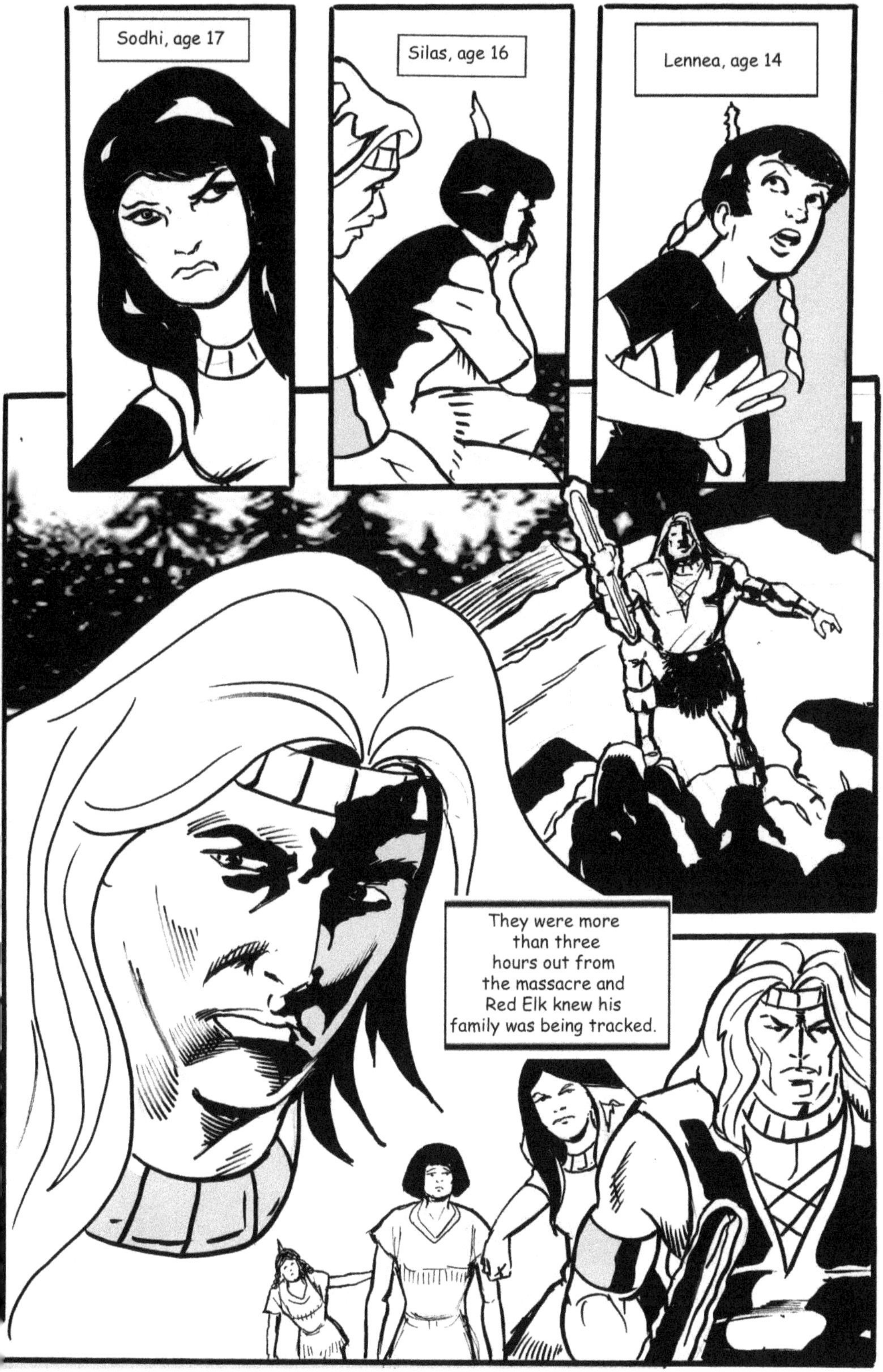
Sodhi, age 17
Silas, age 16
Lennea, age 14
They were more than three hours out from the massacre and Red Elk knew his family was being tracked.

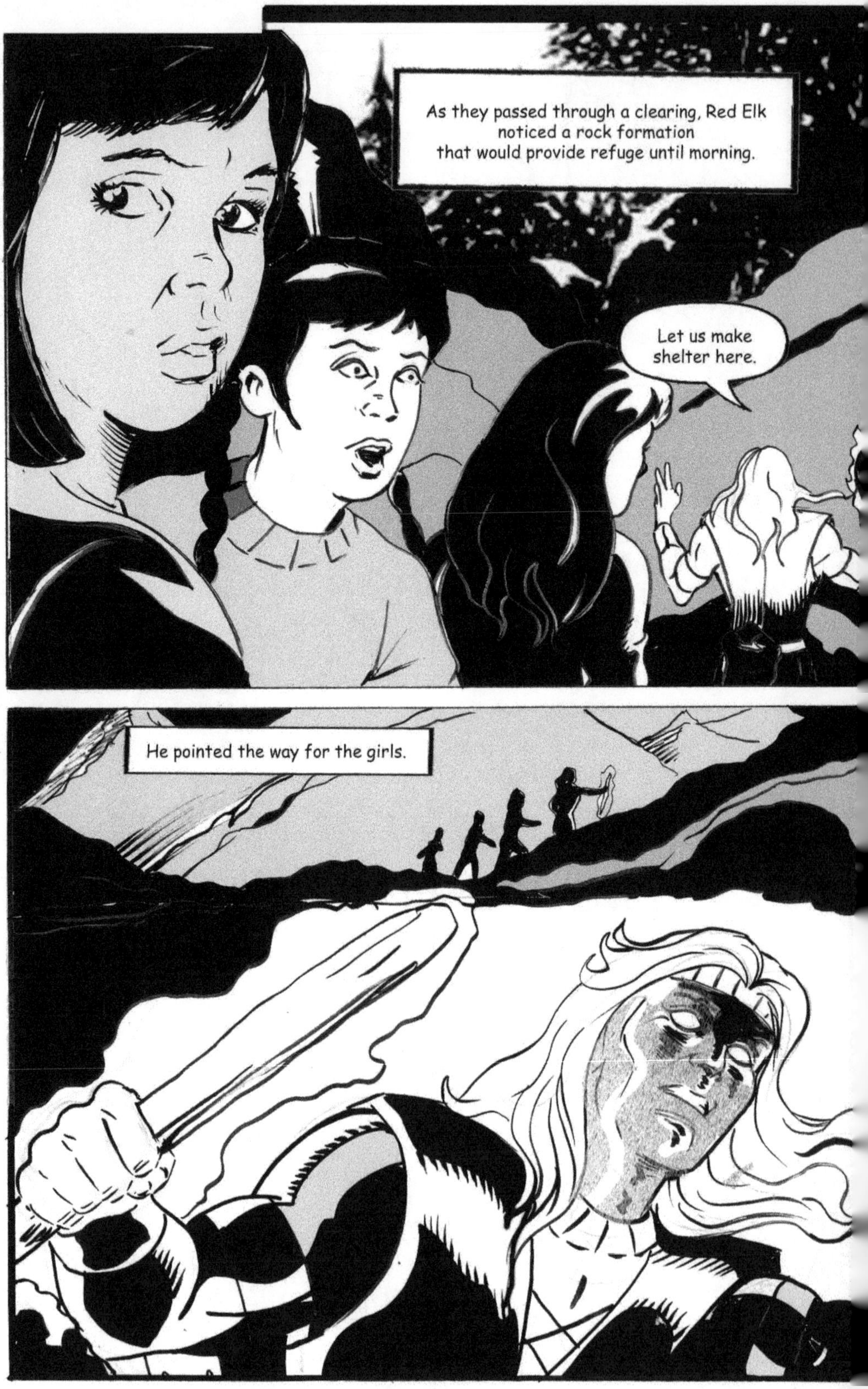
As they passed through a clearing, Red Elk noticed a rock formation that would provide refuge until morning.
Let us make shelter here.
He pointed the way for the girls.

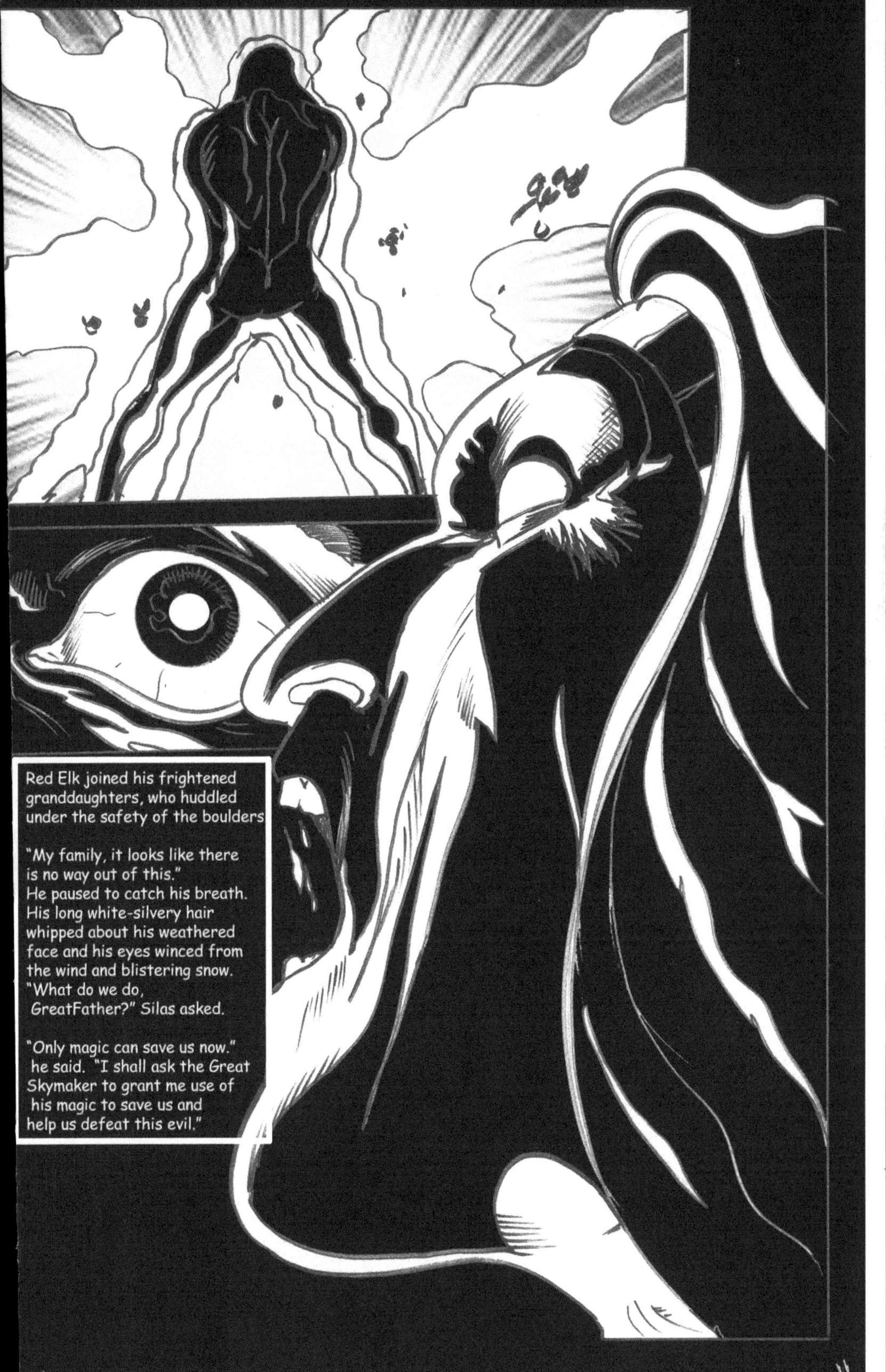
Red Elk joined his frightened granddaughters, who huddled under the safety of the boulders
"My family, it looks like there is no way out of this."
He paused to catch his breath. His long white-silvery hair whipped about his weathered face and his eyes winced from the wind and blistering snow.
"What do we do, GreatFather?" Silas asked.
"Only magic can save us now." he said. "I shall ask the Great Skymaker to grant me use of his magic to save us and help us defeat this evil."

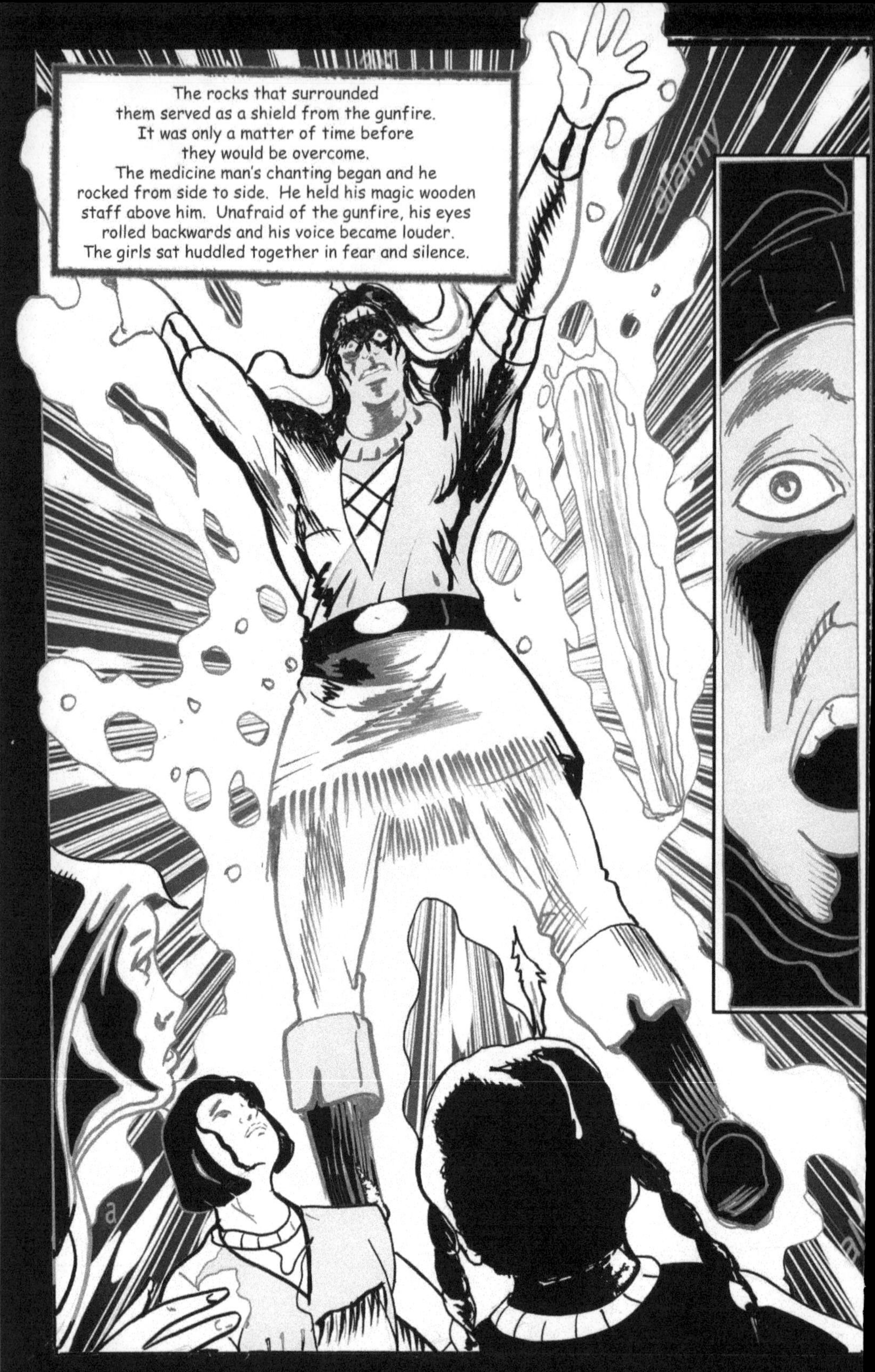
The rocks that surrounded them served as a shield from the gunfire. It was only a matter of time before they would be overcome. The medicine man's chanting began and he rocked from side to side. He held his magic wooden staff above him. Unafraid of the gunfire, his eyes rolled backwards and his voice became louder. The girls sat huddled together in fear and silence.

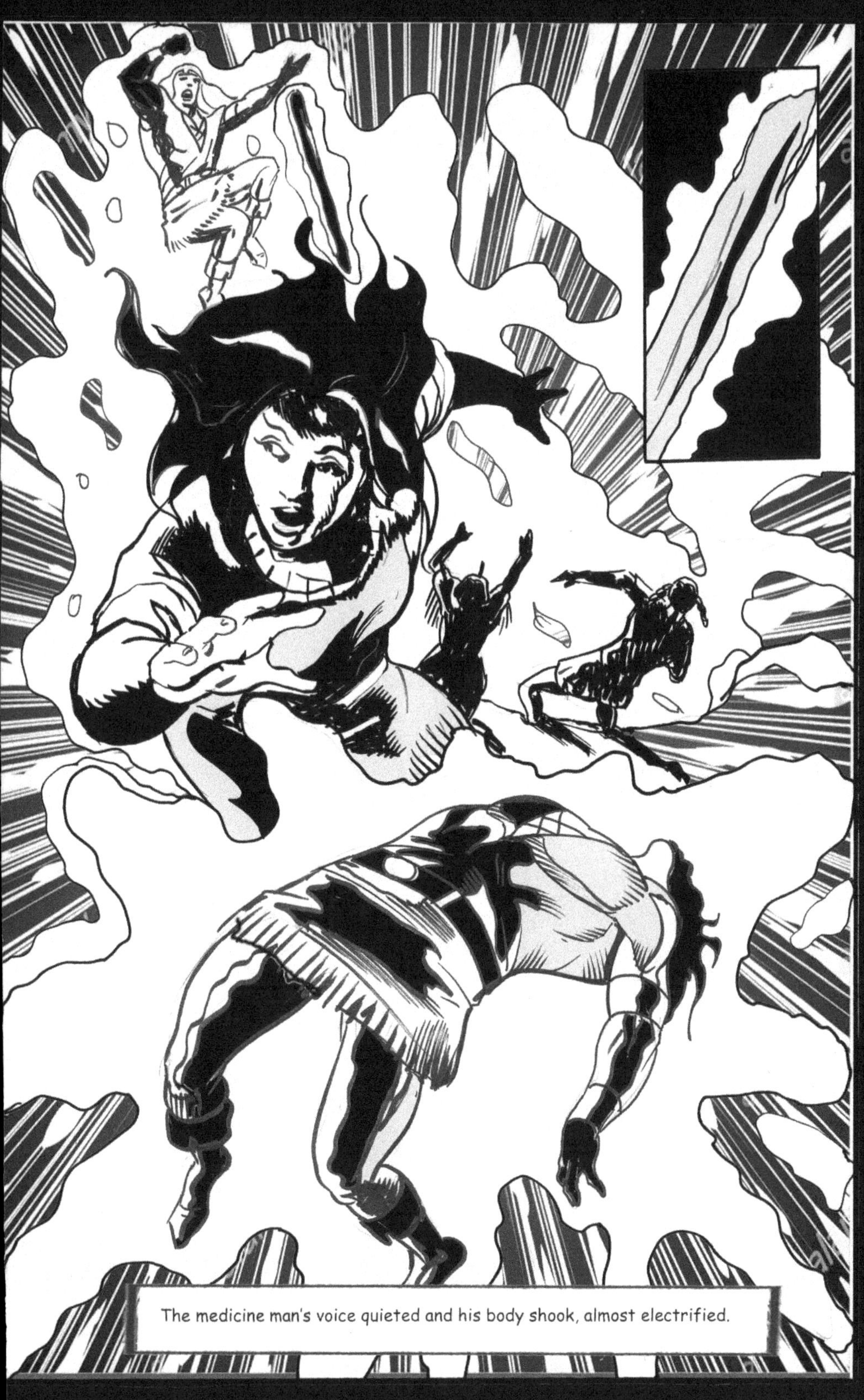
The medicine man's voice quieted and his body shook, almost electrified.

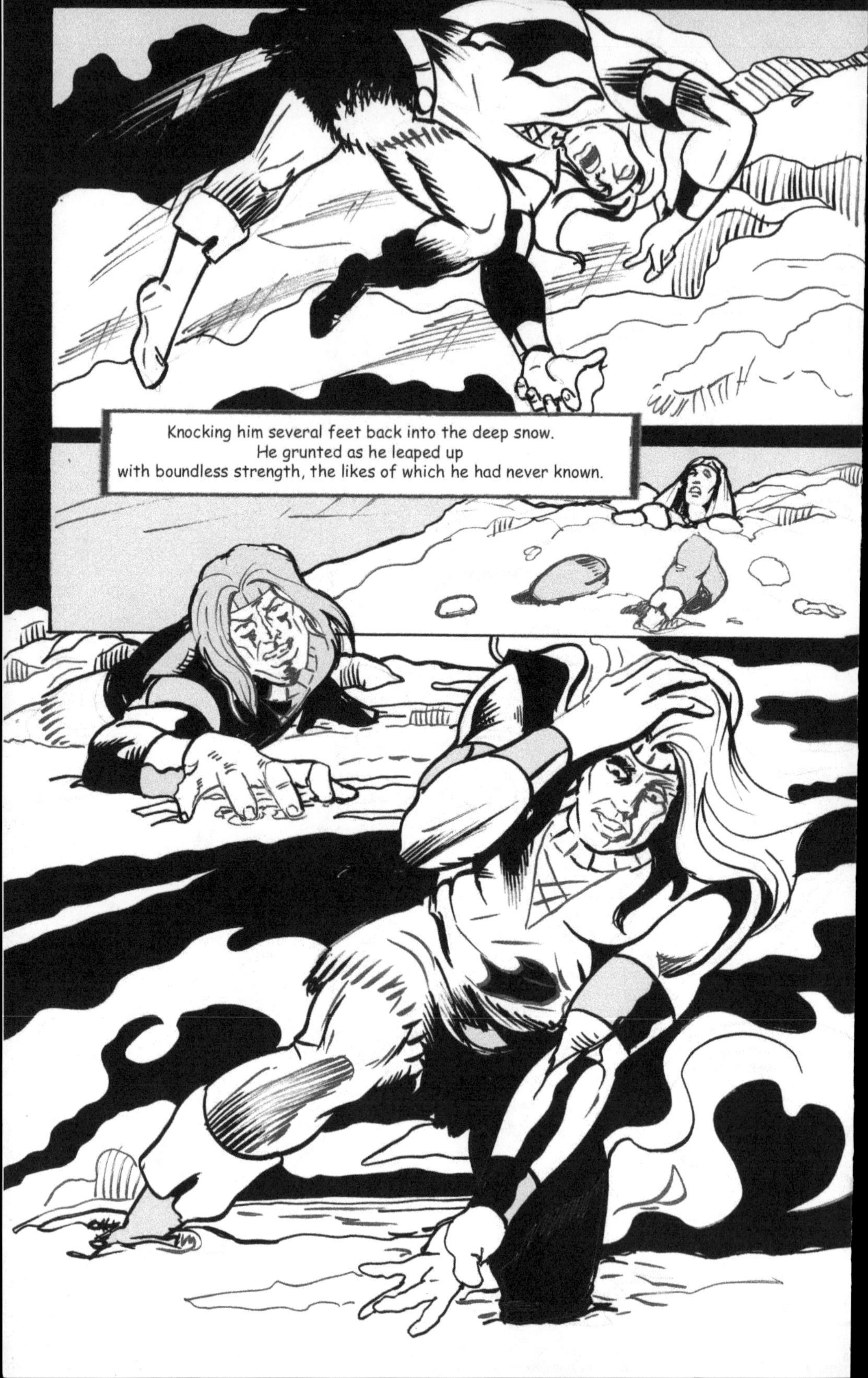
Knocking him several feet back into the deep snow.
He grunted as he leaped up
with boundless strength, the likes of which he had never known.

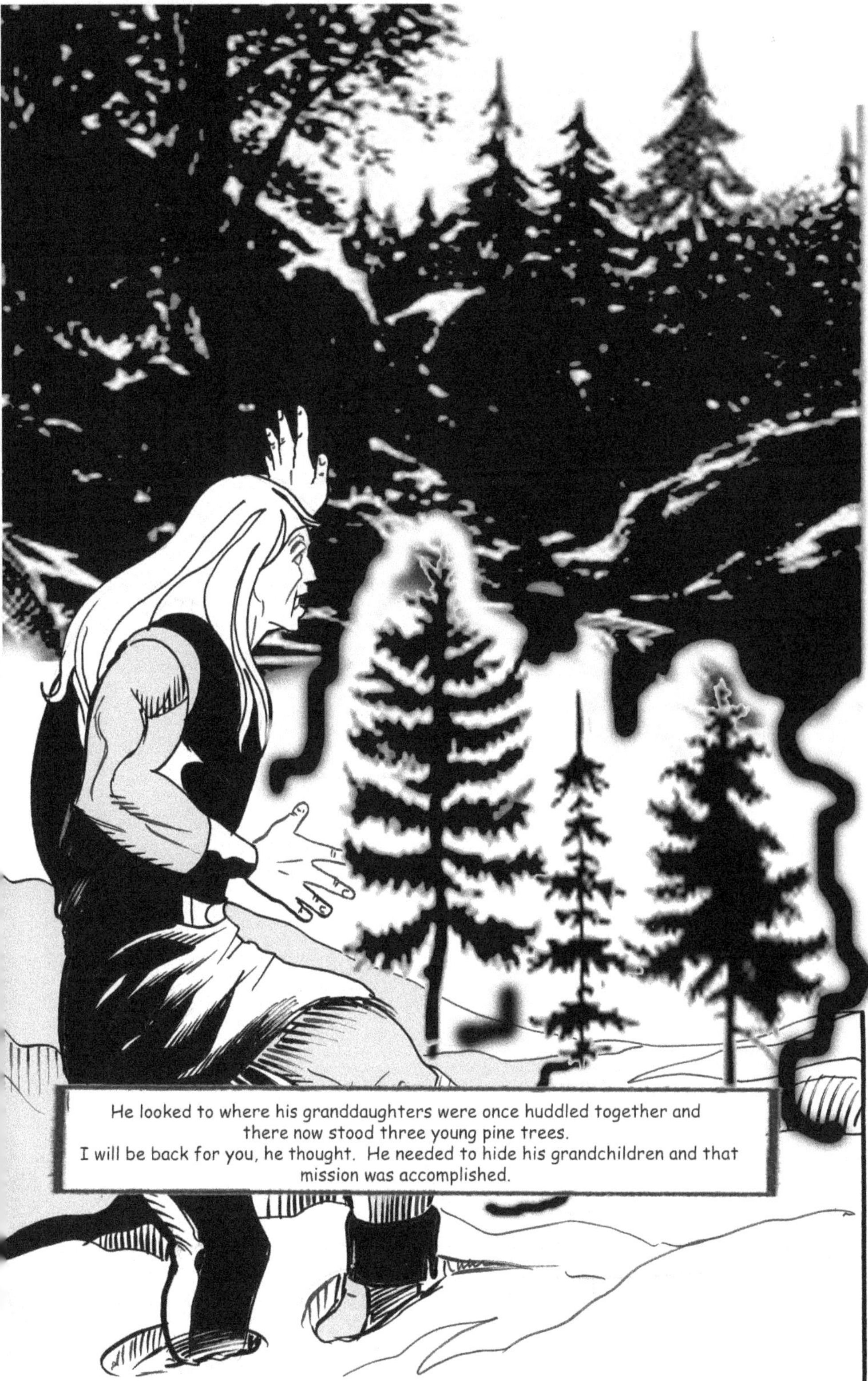
He looked to where his granddaughters were once huddled together and
there now stood three young pine trees.
I will be back for you, he thought. He needed to hide his grandchildren and that
mission was accomplished.

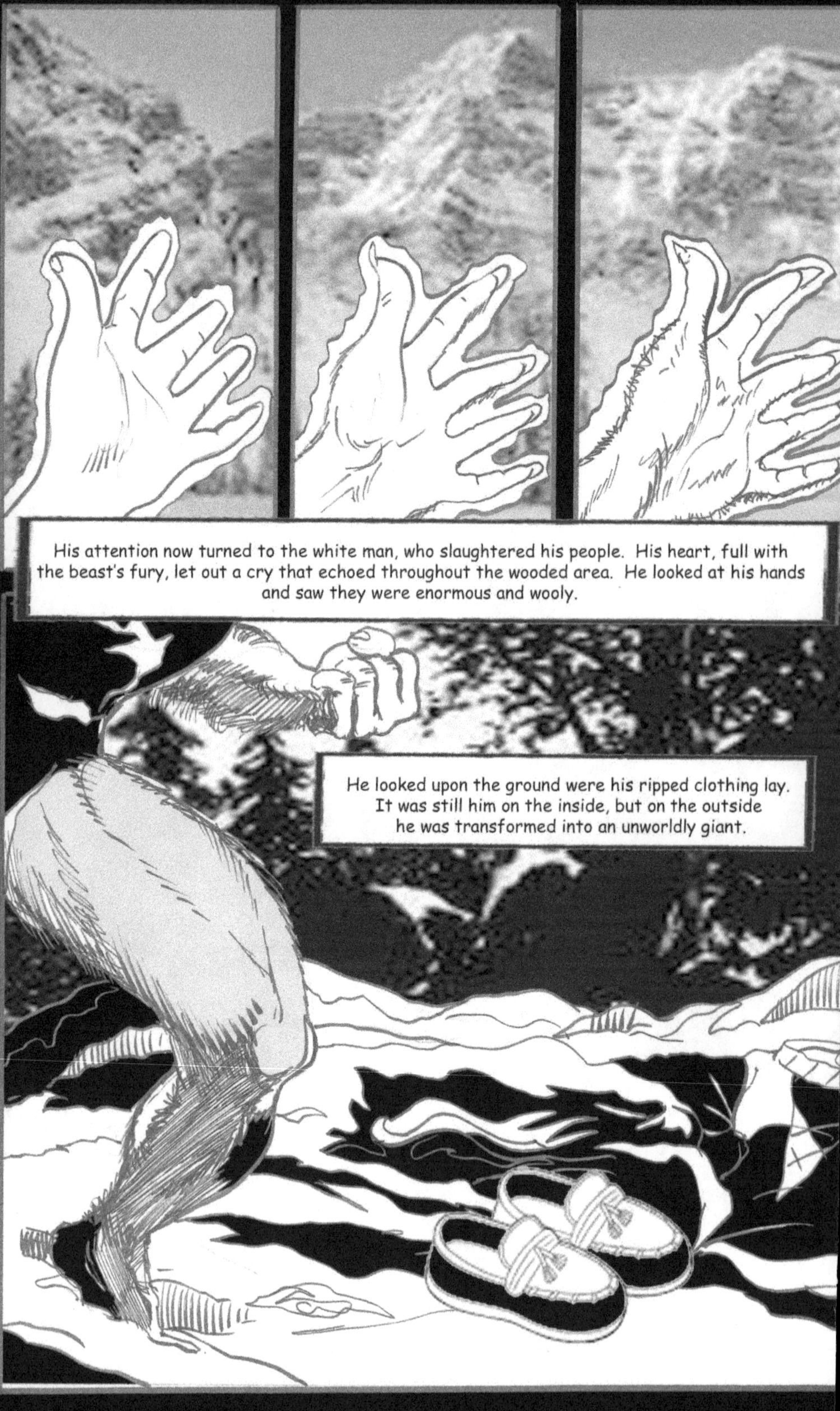
His attention now turned to the white man, who slaughtered his people. His heart, full with the beast's fury, let out a cry that echoed throughout the wooded area. He looked at his hands and saw they were enormous and wooly.
He looked upon the ground were his ripped clothing lay. It was still him on the inside, but on the outside he was transformed into an unworldly giant.

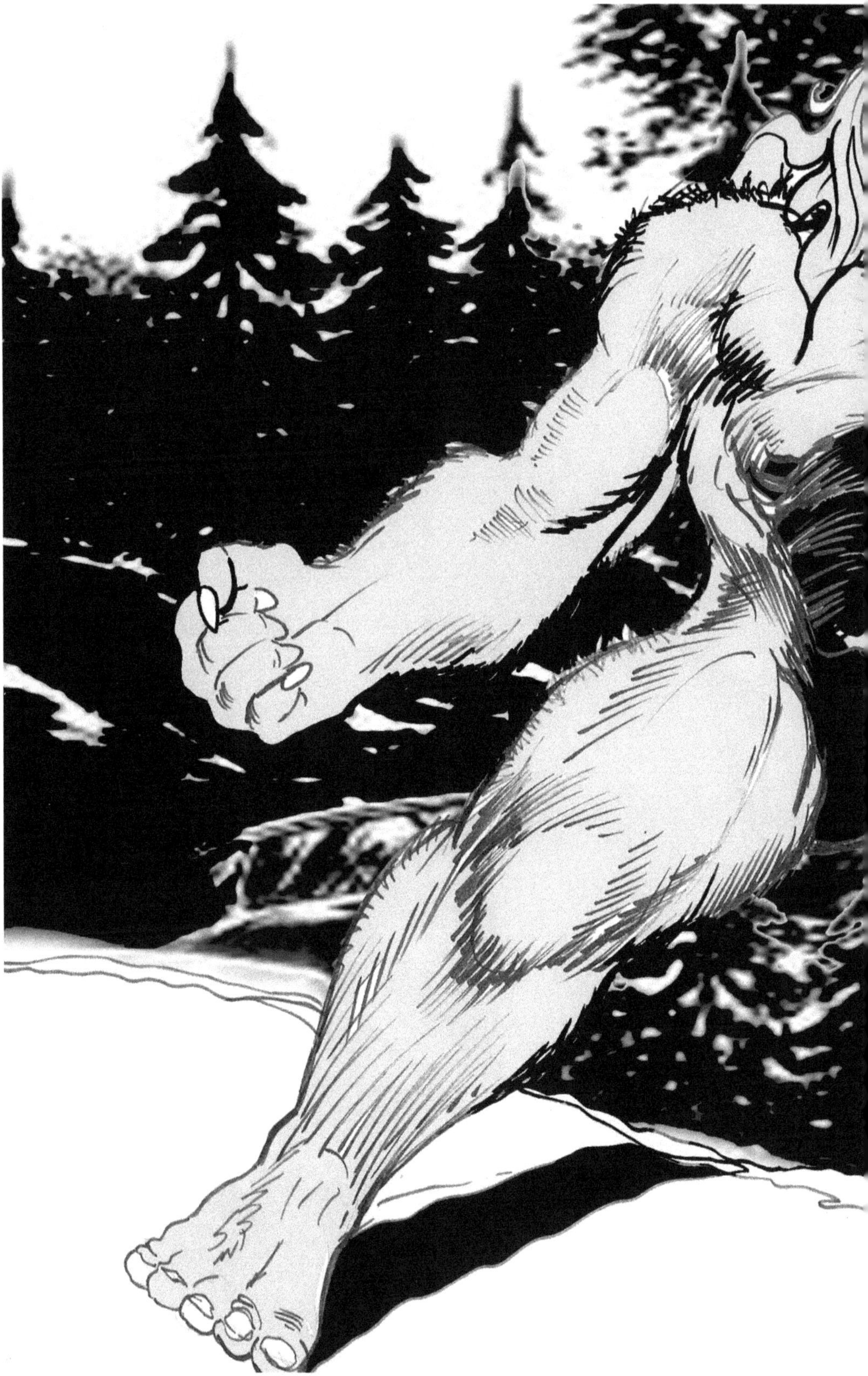

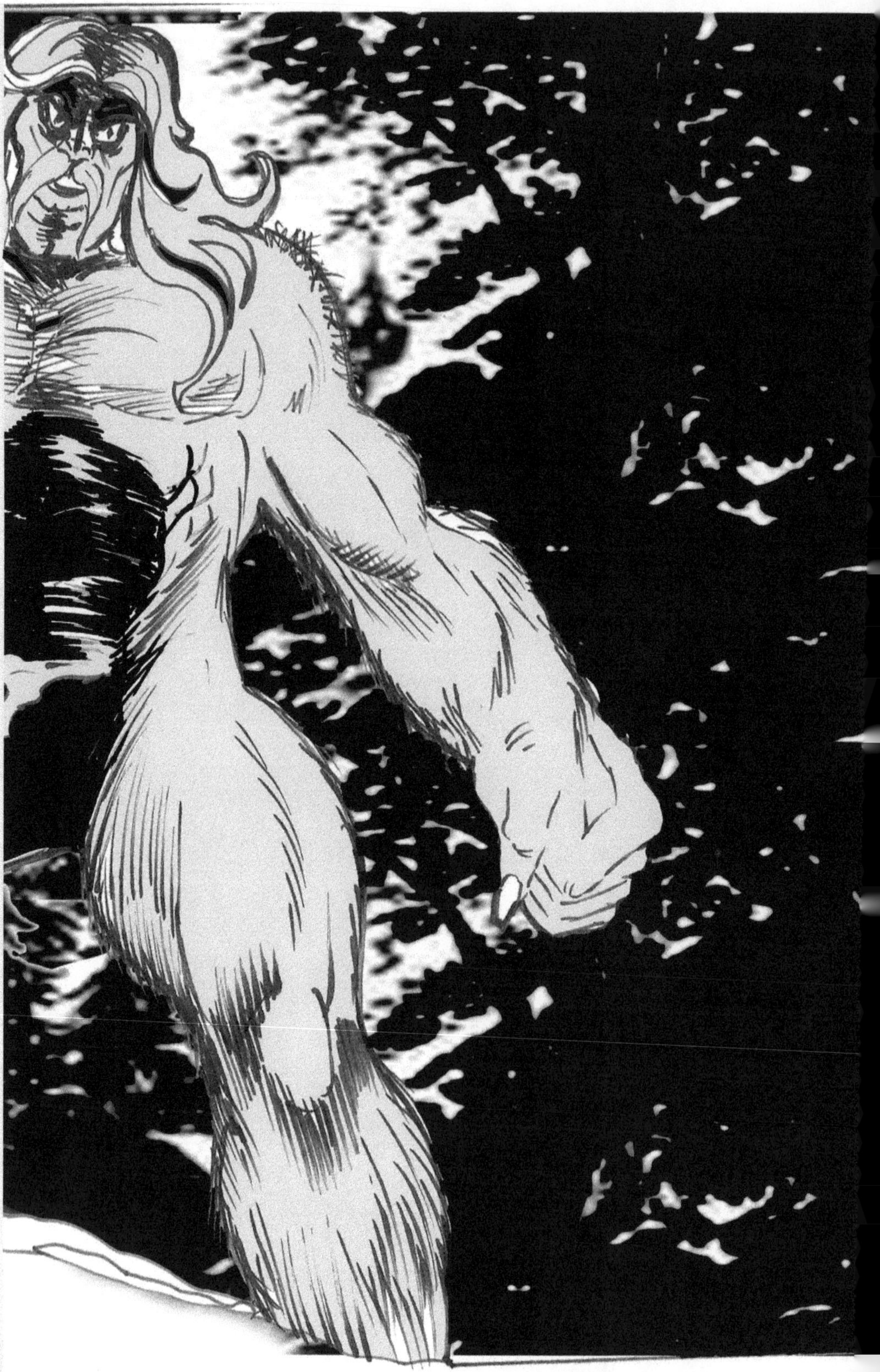

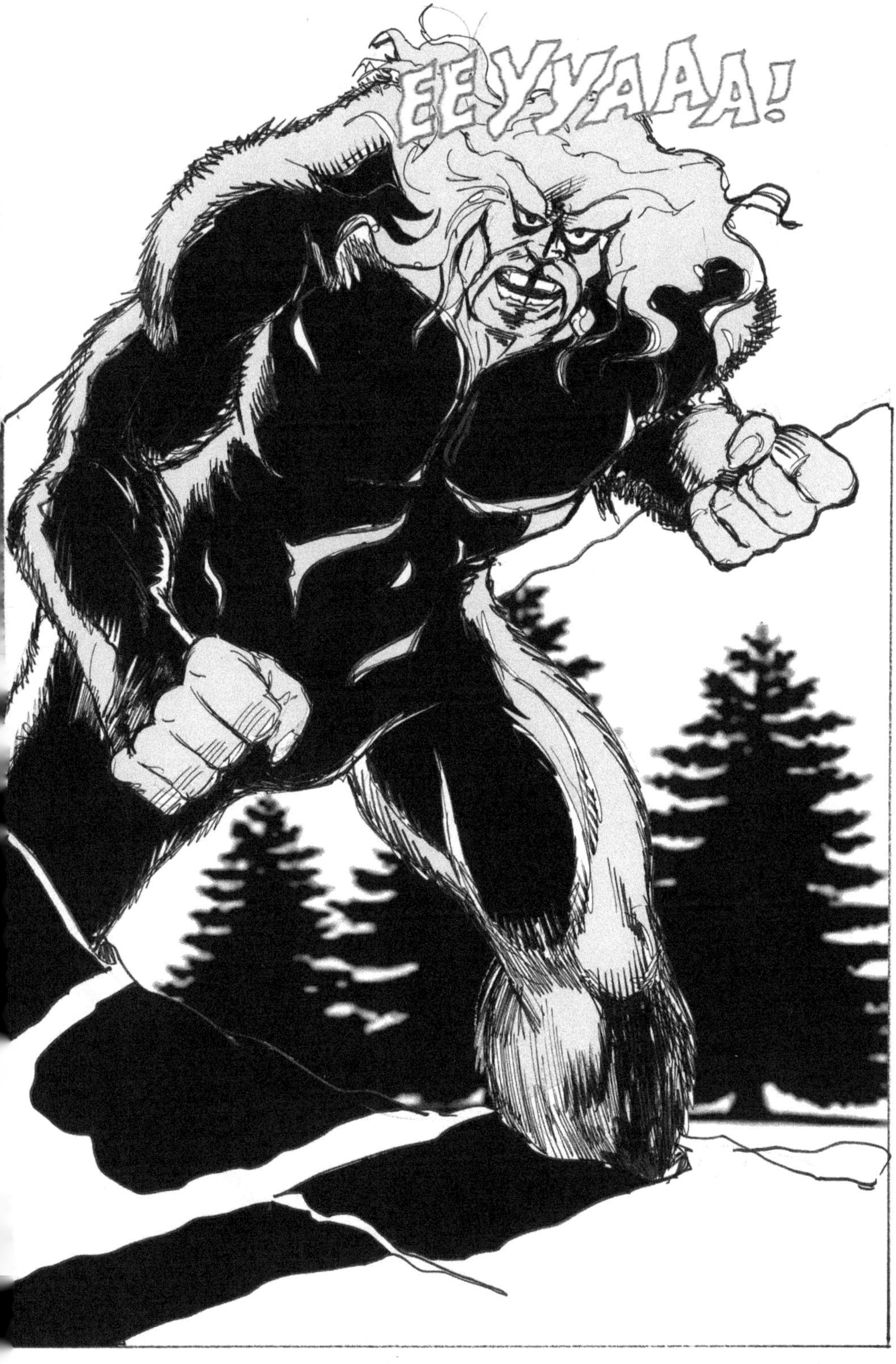
EEYYAAA!

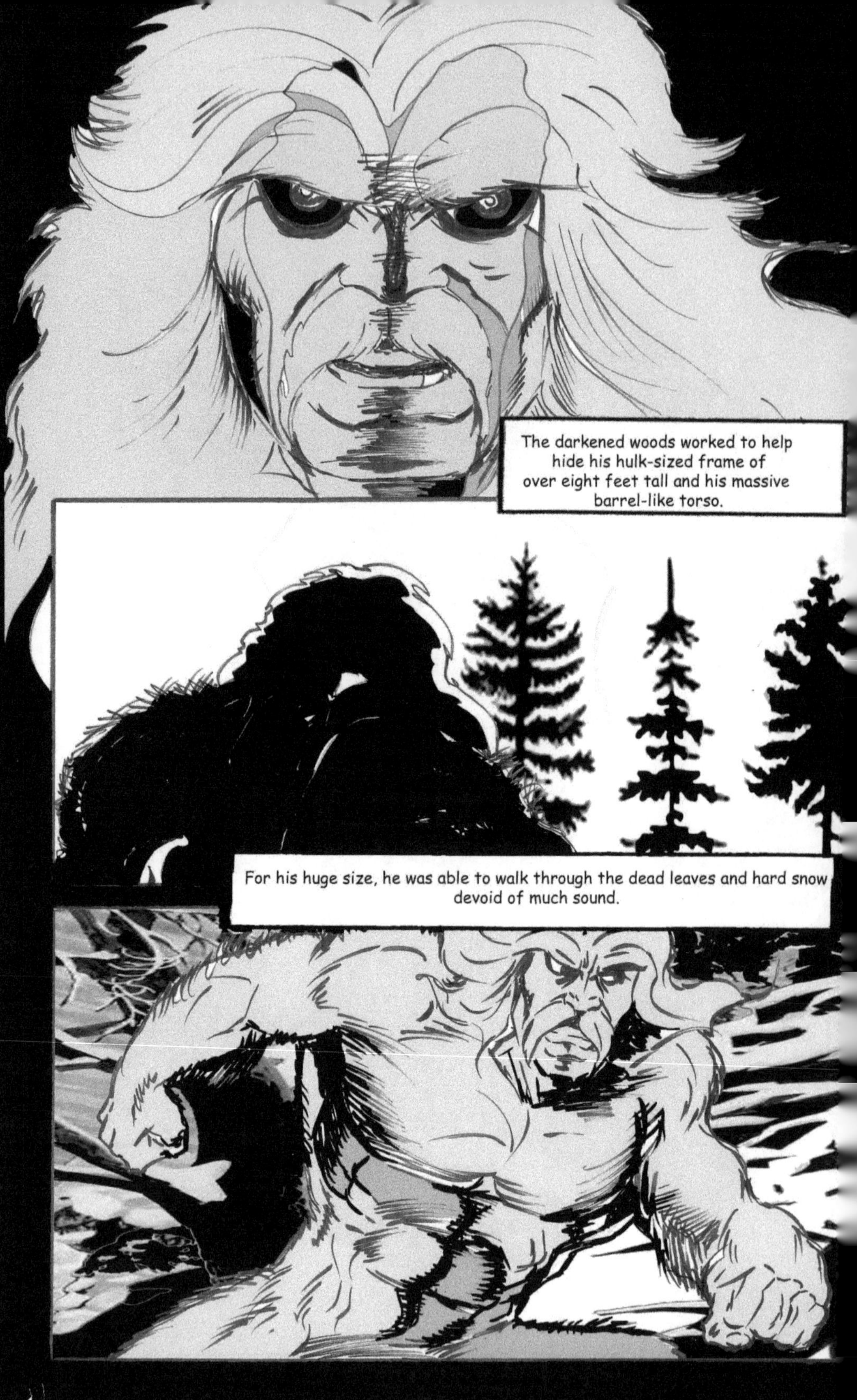
The darkened woods worked to help hide his hulk-sized frame of over eight feet tall and his massive barrel-like torso.
For his huge size, he was able to walk through the dead leaves and hard snow devoid of much sound.

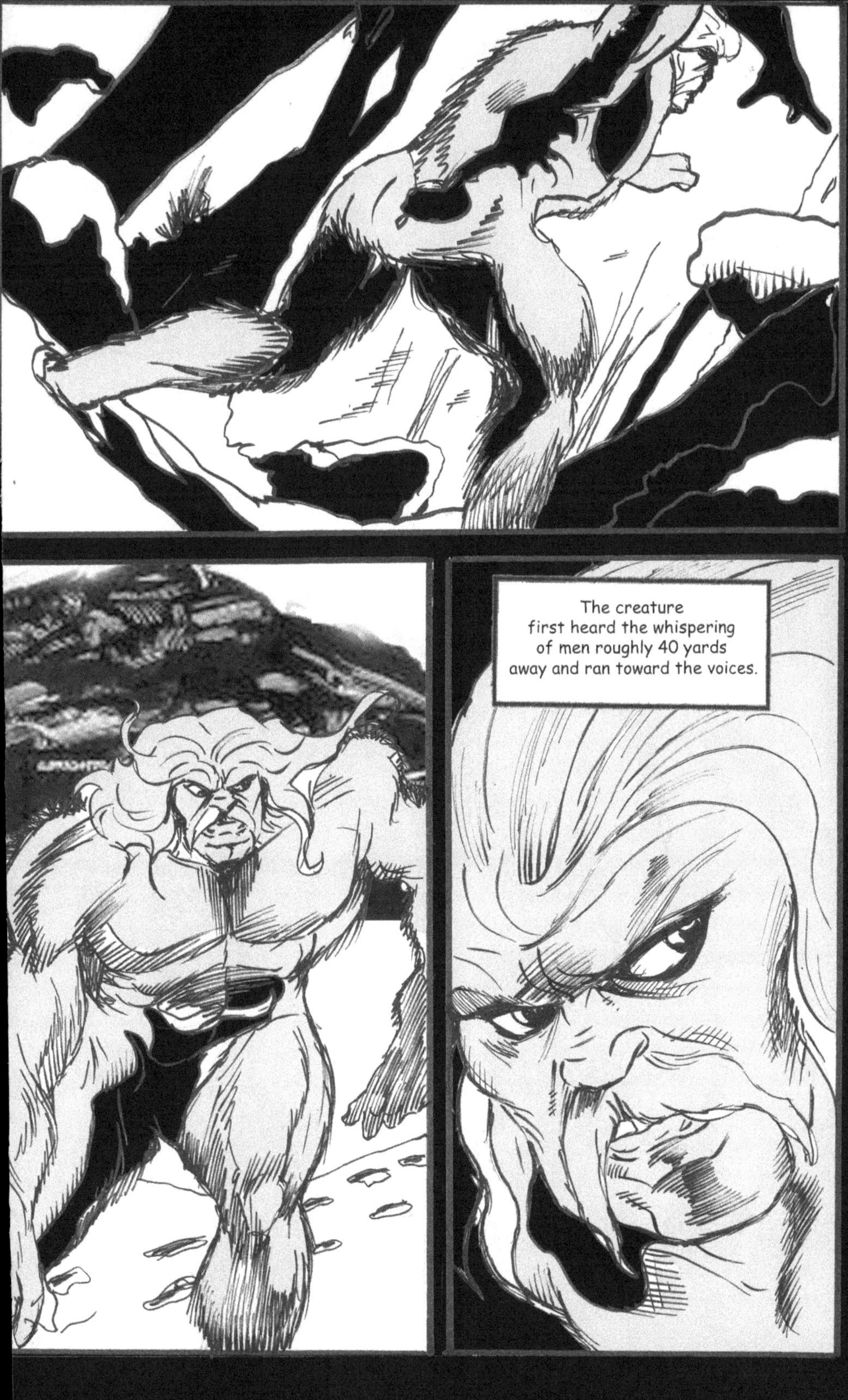
The creature first heard the whispering of men roughly 40 yards away and ran toward the voices.

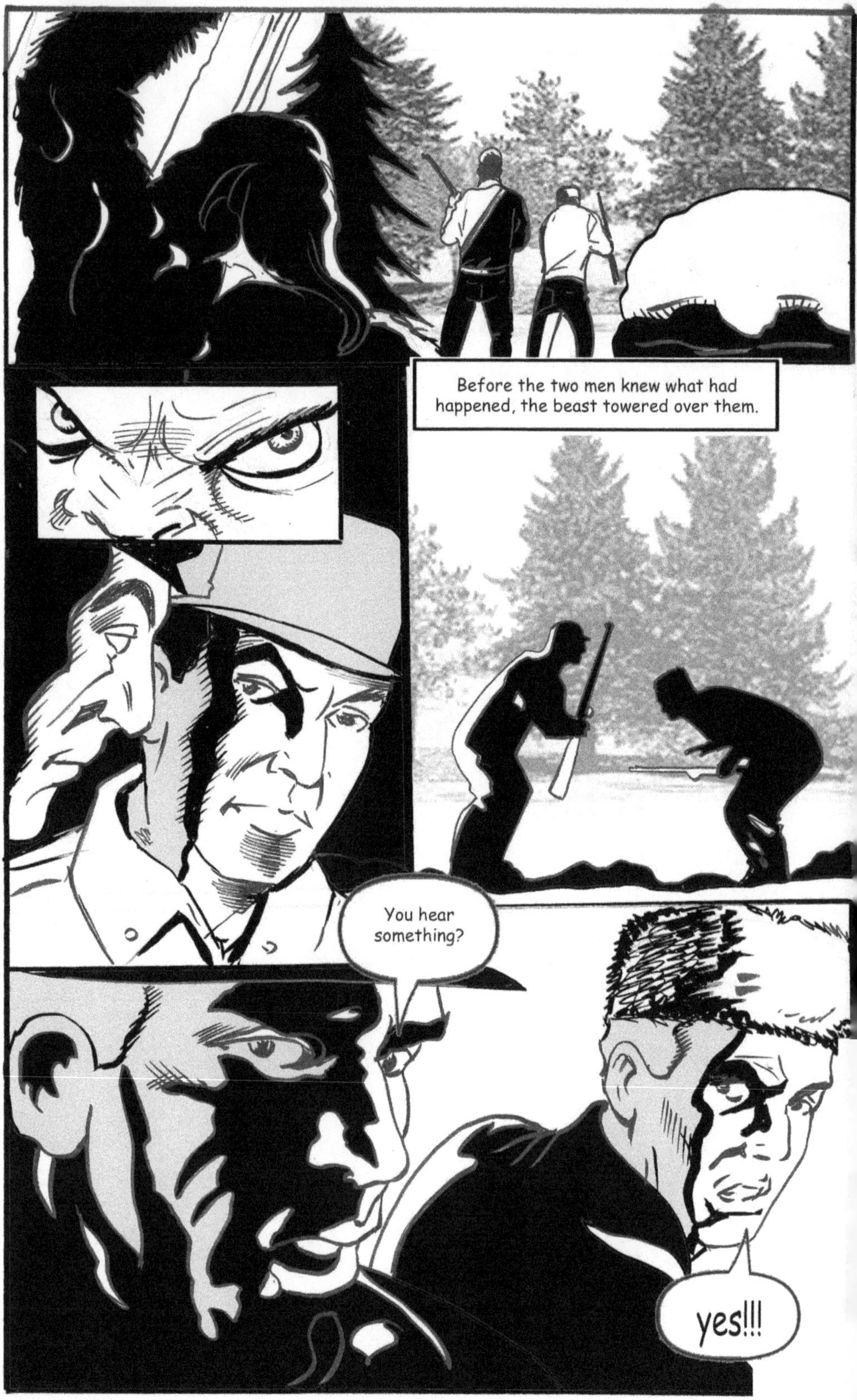
Before the two men knew what had happened, the beast towered over them.
You hear something?
yes!!!

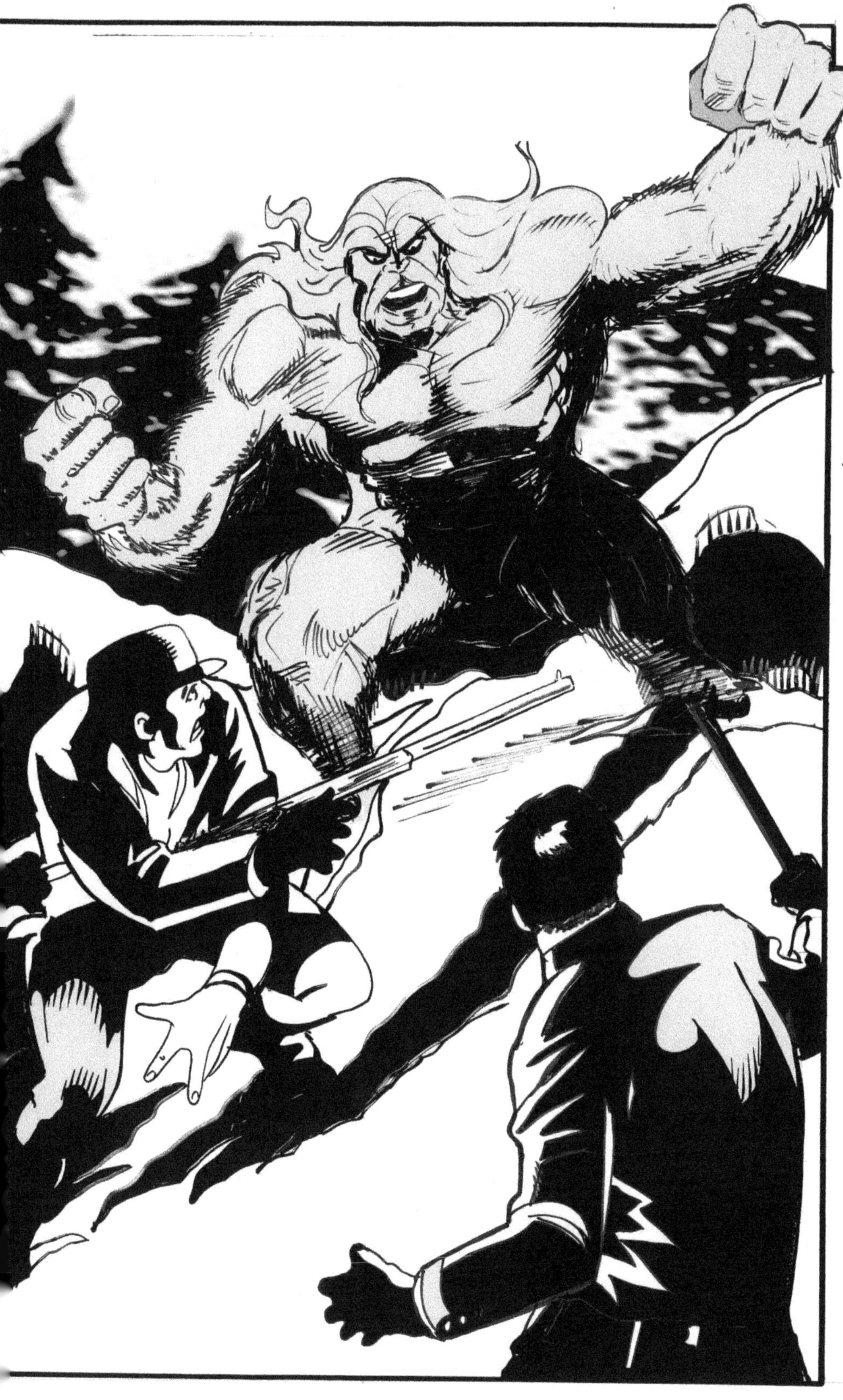

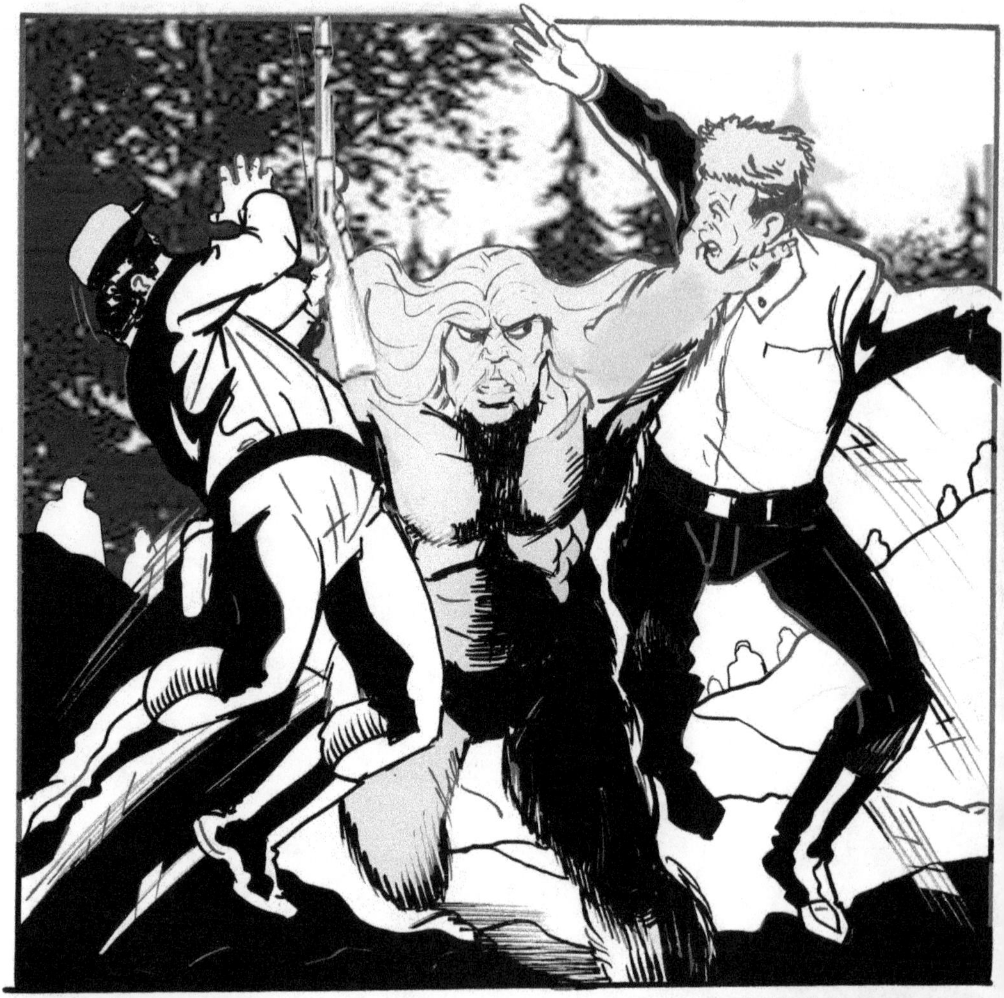

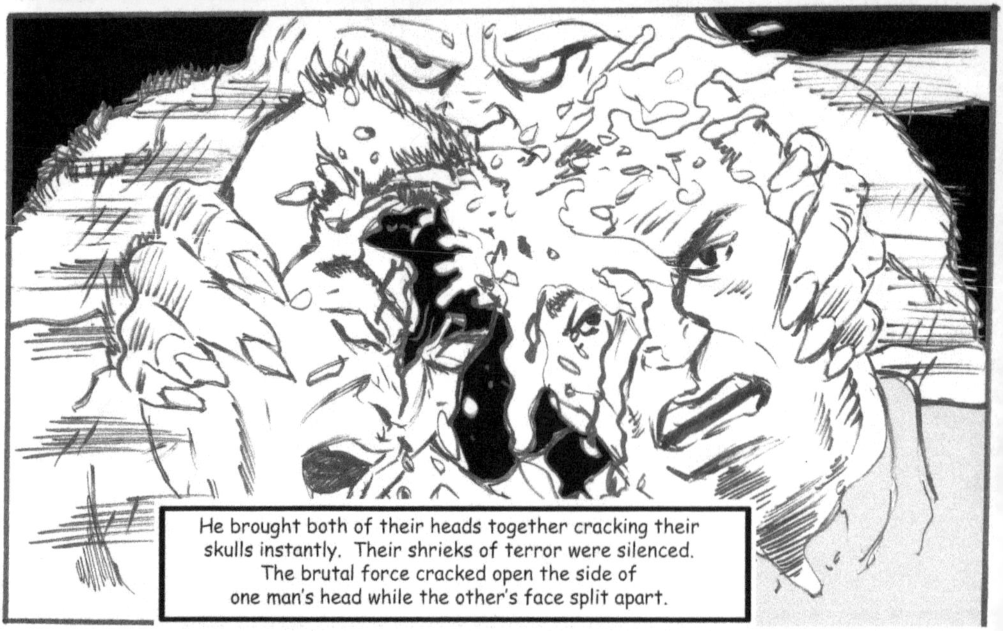
He brought both of their heads together cracking their skulls instantly. Their shrieks of terror were silenced. The brutal force cracked open the side of one man's head while the other's face split apart.

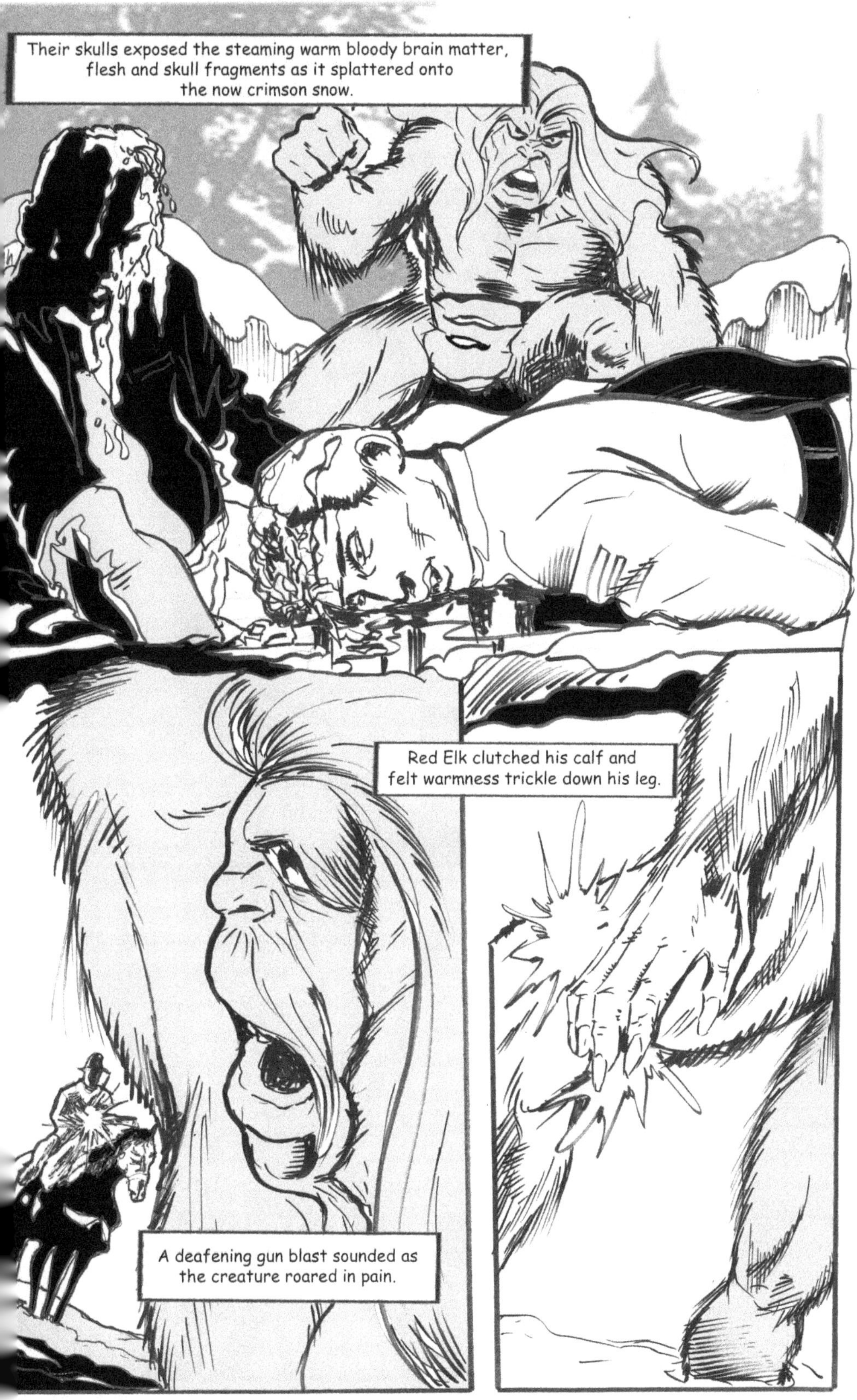
Their skulls exposed the steaming warm bloody brain matter, flesh and skull fragments as it splattered onto the now crimson snow.
Red Elk clutched his calf and felt warmness trickle down his leg.
A deafening gun blast sounded as the creature roared in pain.

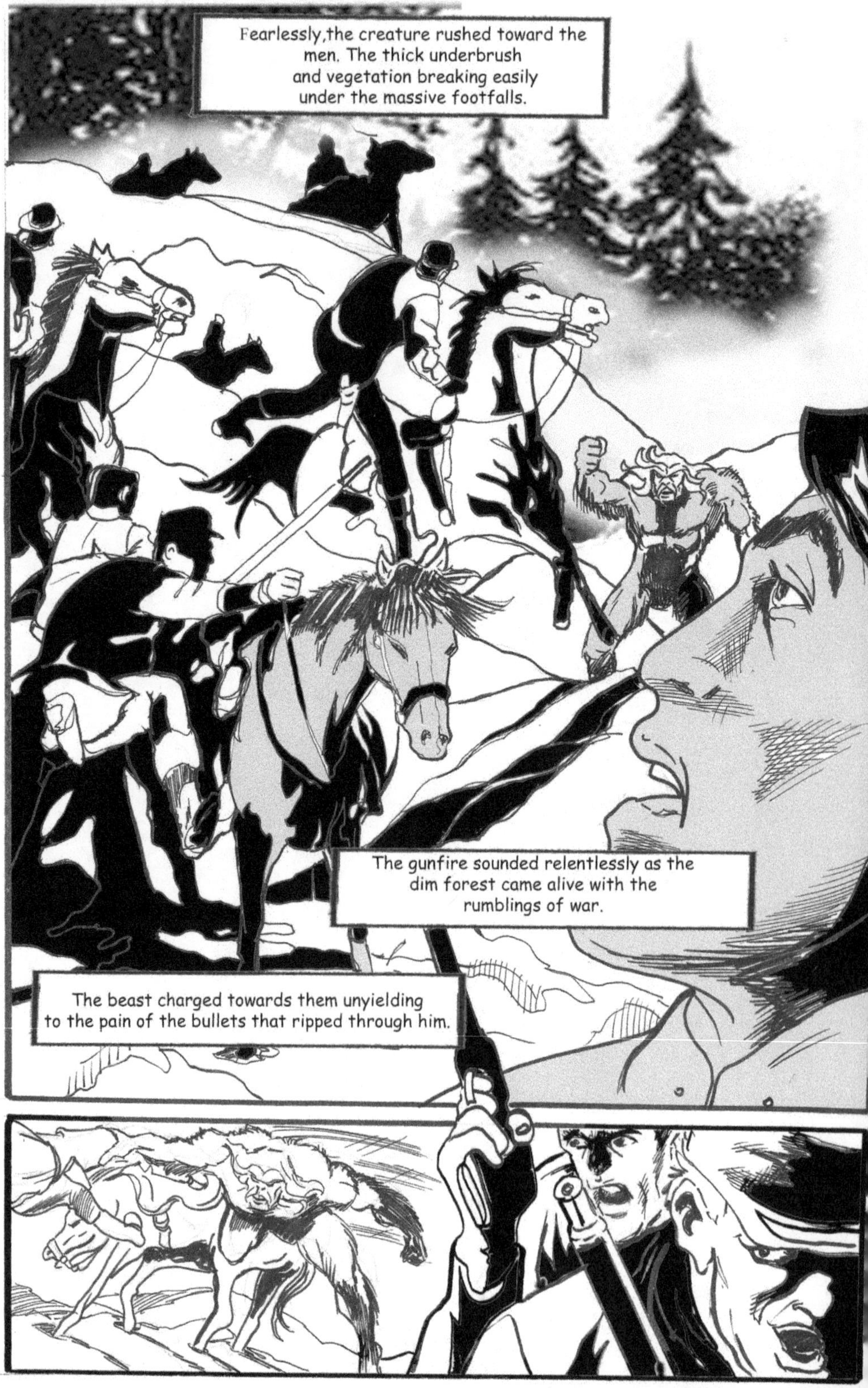
Fearlessly,the creature rushed toward the men. The thick underbrush and vegetation breaking easily under the massive footfalls.
The gunfire sounded relentlessly as the dim forest came alive with the rumblings of war.
The beast charged towards them unyielding to the pain of the bullets that ripped through him.

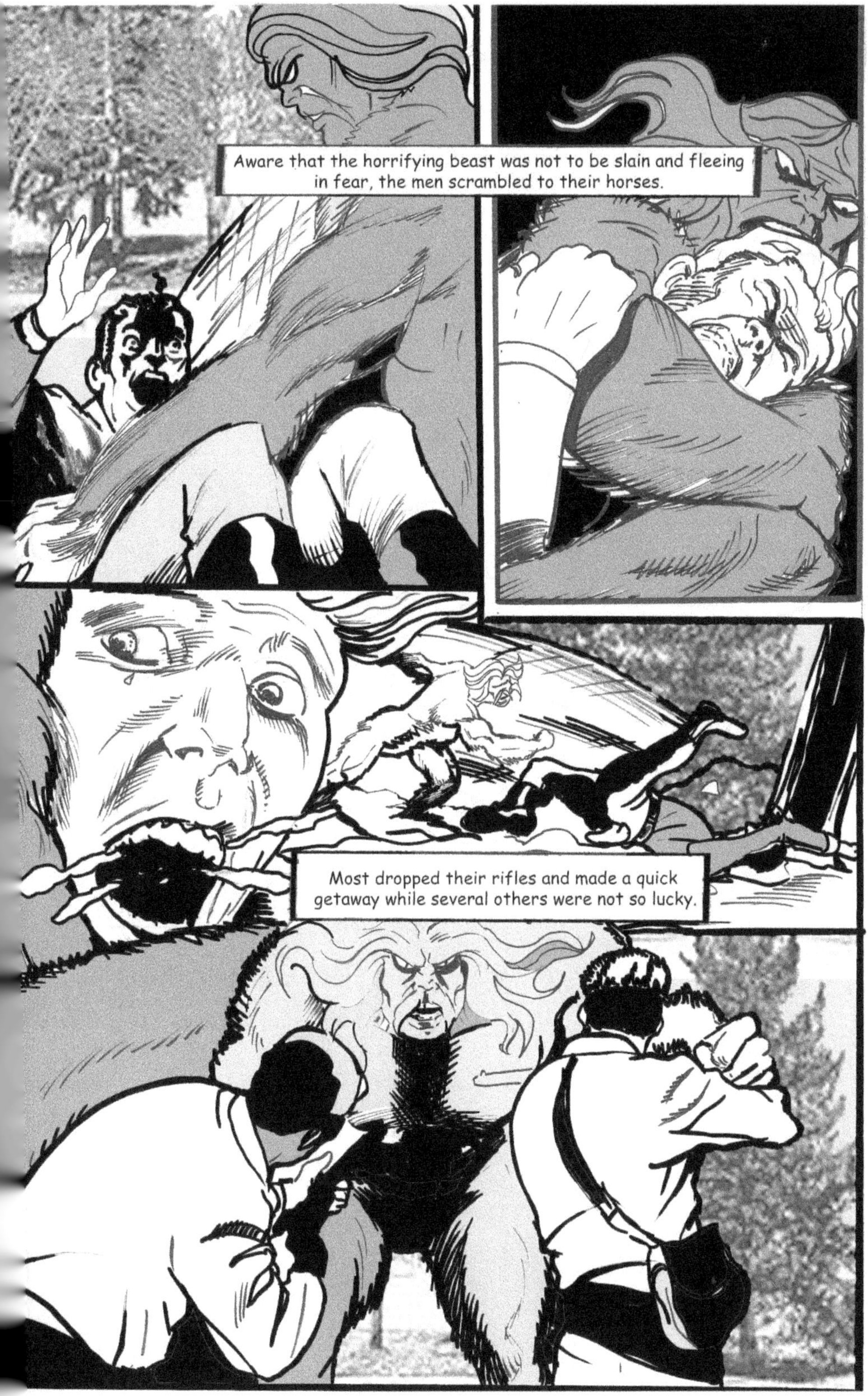
Aware that the horrifying beast was not to be slain and fleeing in fear, the men scrambled to their horses.
Most dropped their rifles and made a quick getaway while several others were not so lucky.

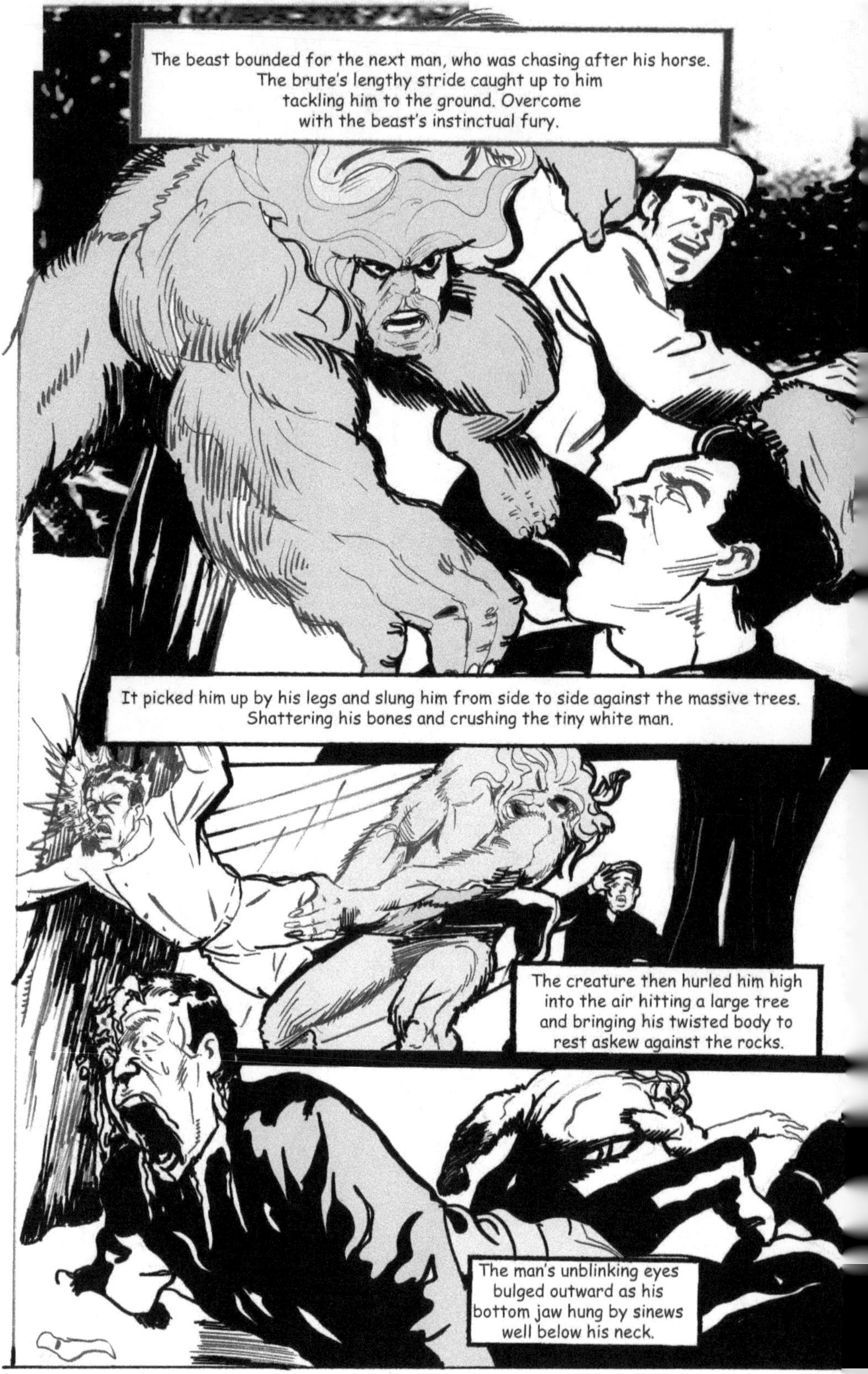
The beast bounded for the next man, who was chasing after his horse. The brute's lengthy stride caught up to him tackling him to the ground. Overcome with the beast's instinctual fury.
It picked him up by his legs and slung him from side to side against the massive trees. Shattering his bones and crushing the tiny white man.
The creature then hurled him high into the air hitting a large tree and bringing his twisted body to rest askew against the rocks.
The man's unblinking eyes bulged outward as his bottom jaw hung by sinews well below his neck.

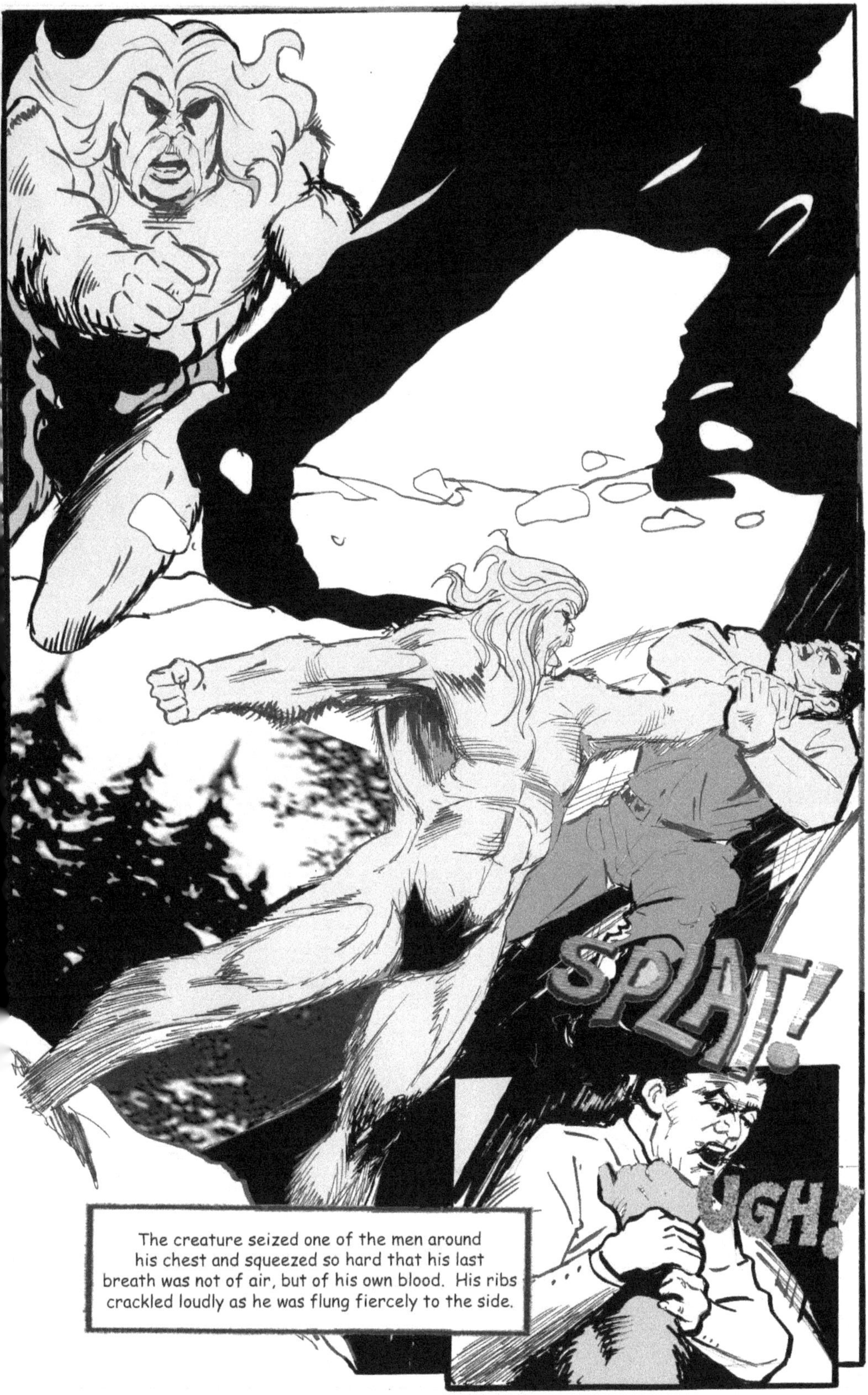
SPLAT!
UGH!
The creature seized one of the men around his chest and squeezed so hard that his last breath was not of air, but of his own blood. His ribs crackled loudly as he was flung fiercely to the side.

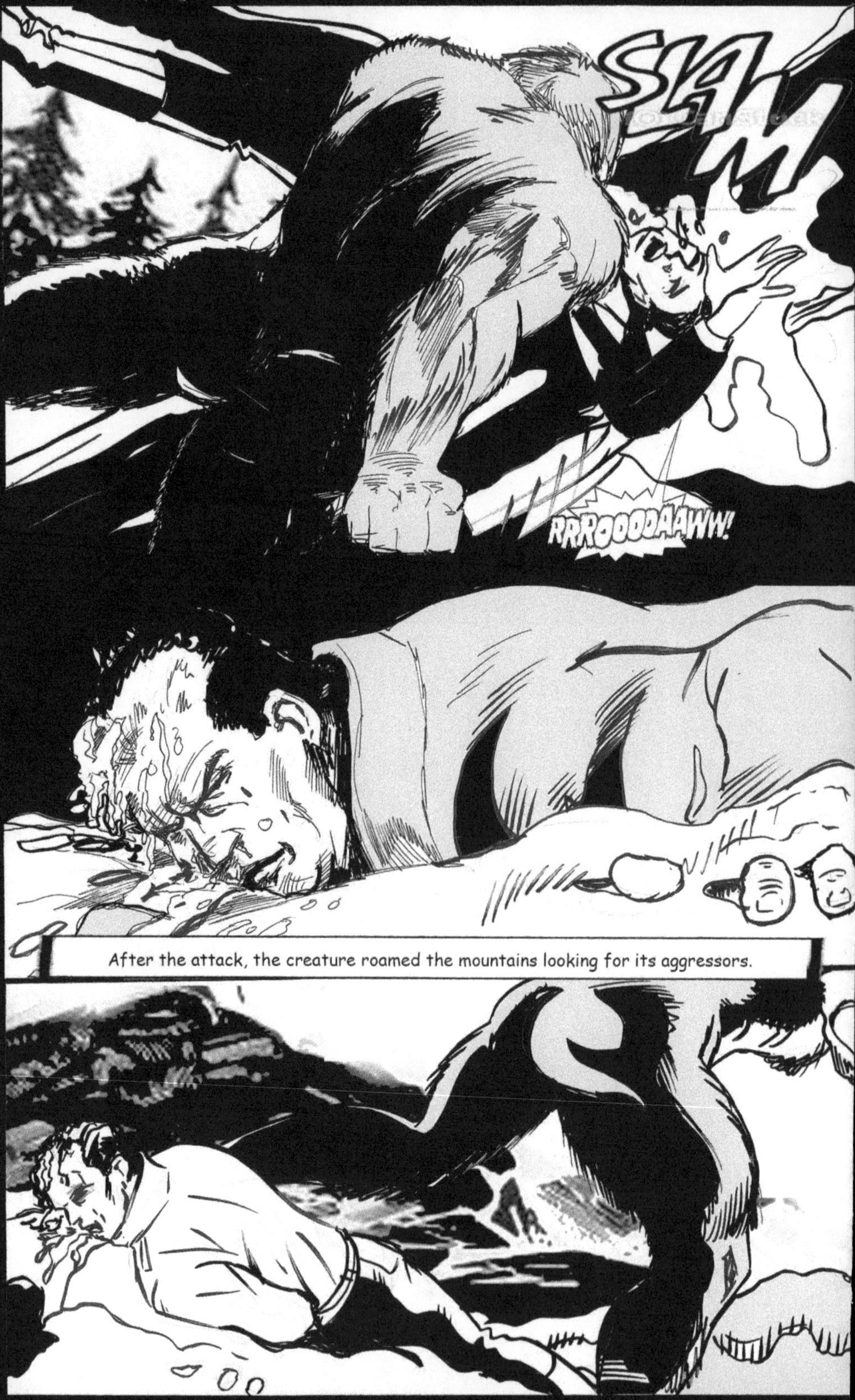
SLAM
RRROOOOAAWW!
After the attack, the creature roamed the mountains looking for its aggressors.

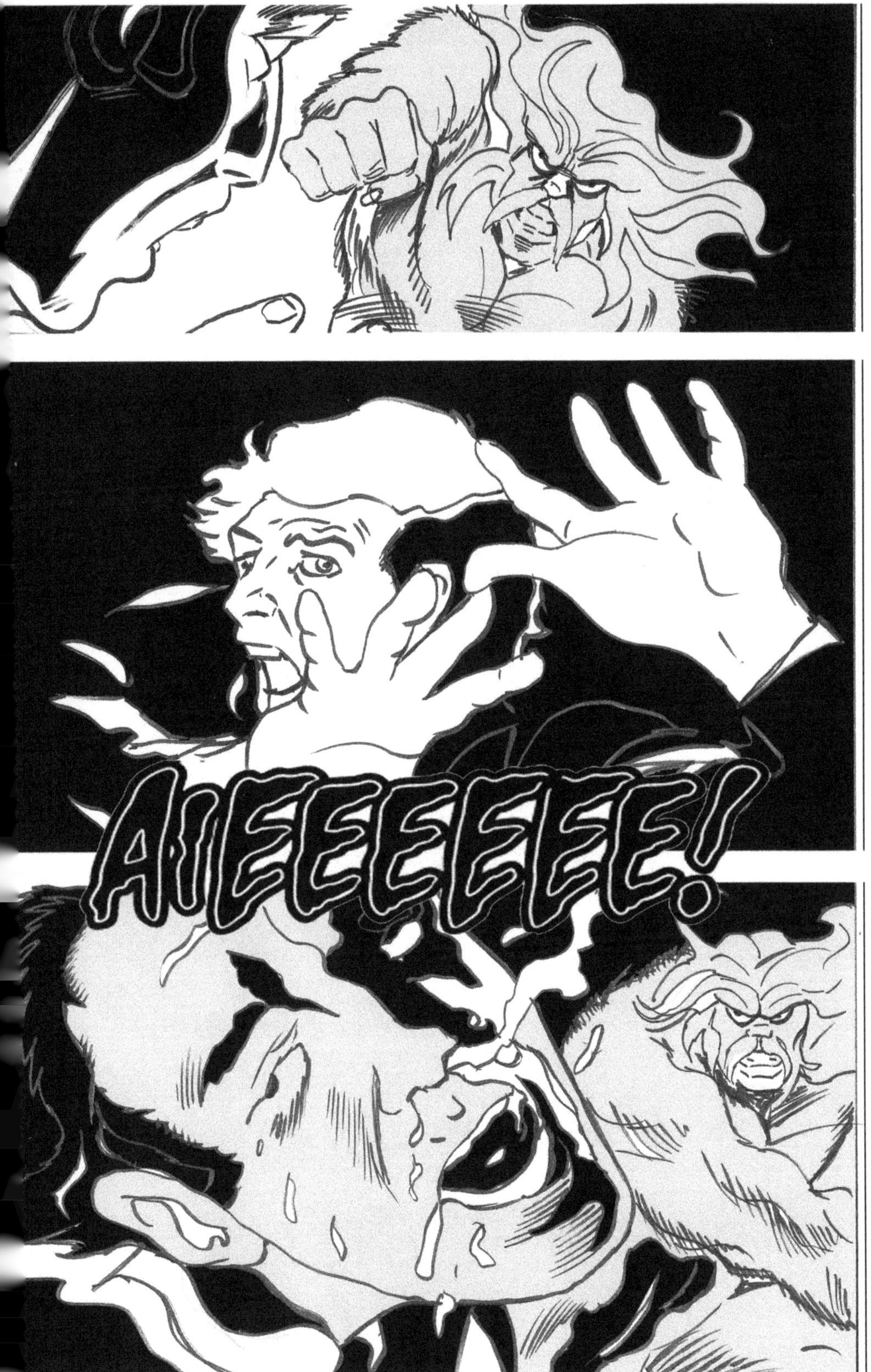
AIEEEEEEE!

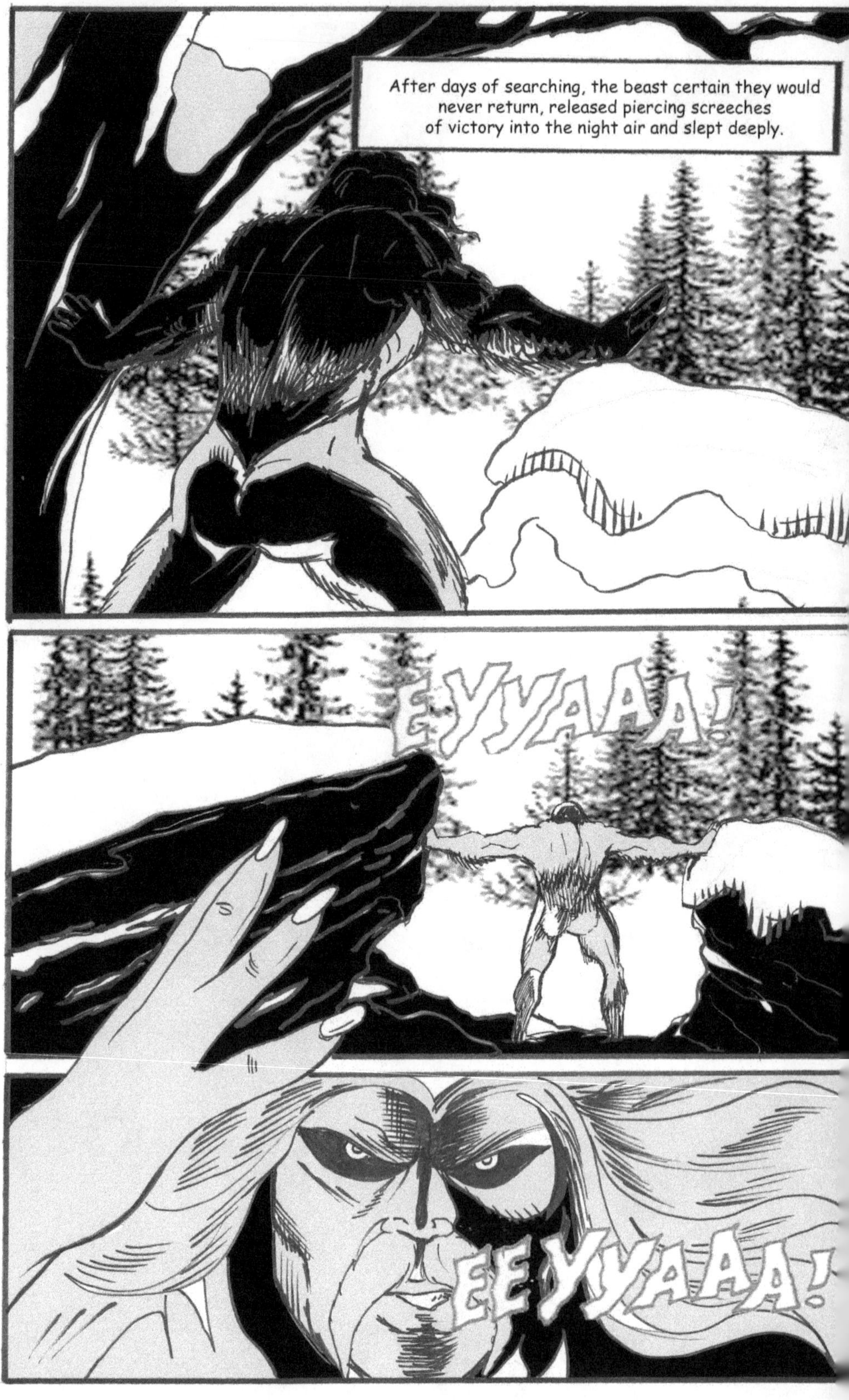
After days of searching, the beast certain they would never return, released piercing screeches of victory into the night air and slept deeply.
EYYAAA!
EEYYAAA!

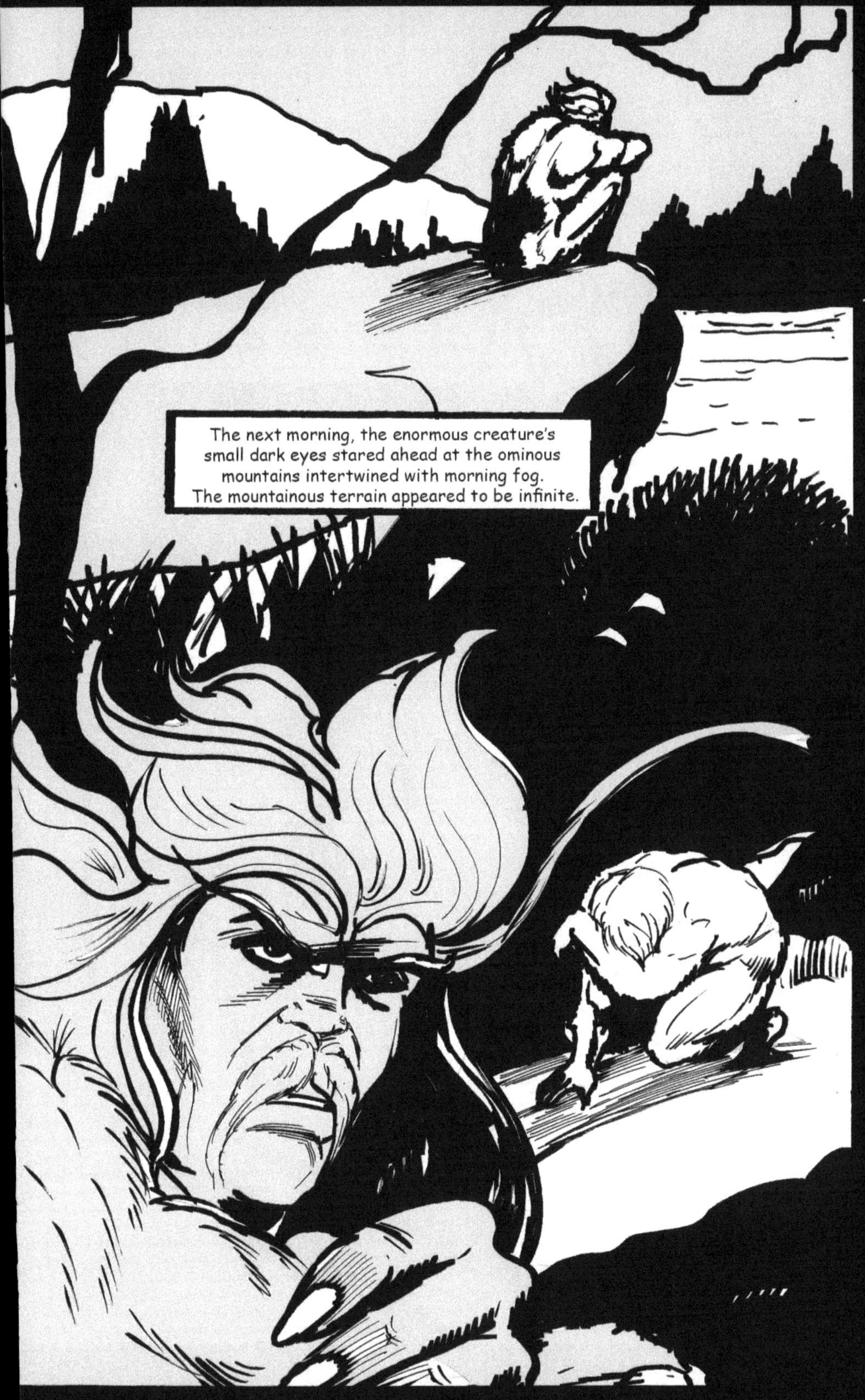
The next morning, the enormous creature's small dark eyes stared ahead at the ominous mountains intertwined with morning fog. The mountainous terrain appeared to be infinite.

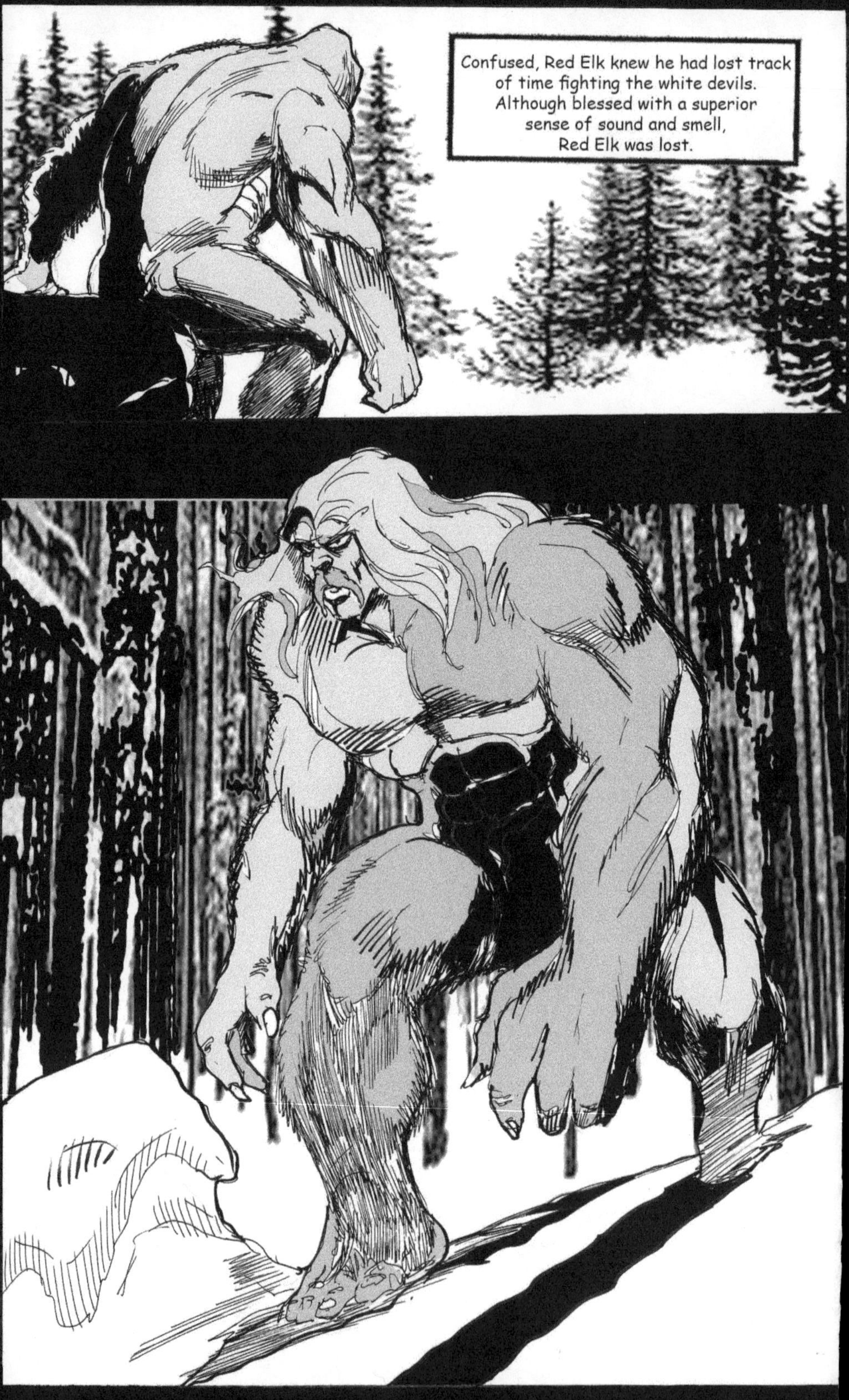
Confused, Red Elk knew he had lost track of time fighting the white devils. Although blessed with a superior sense of sound and smell, Red Elk was lost.

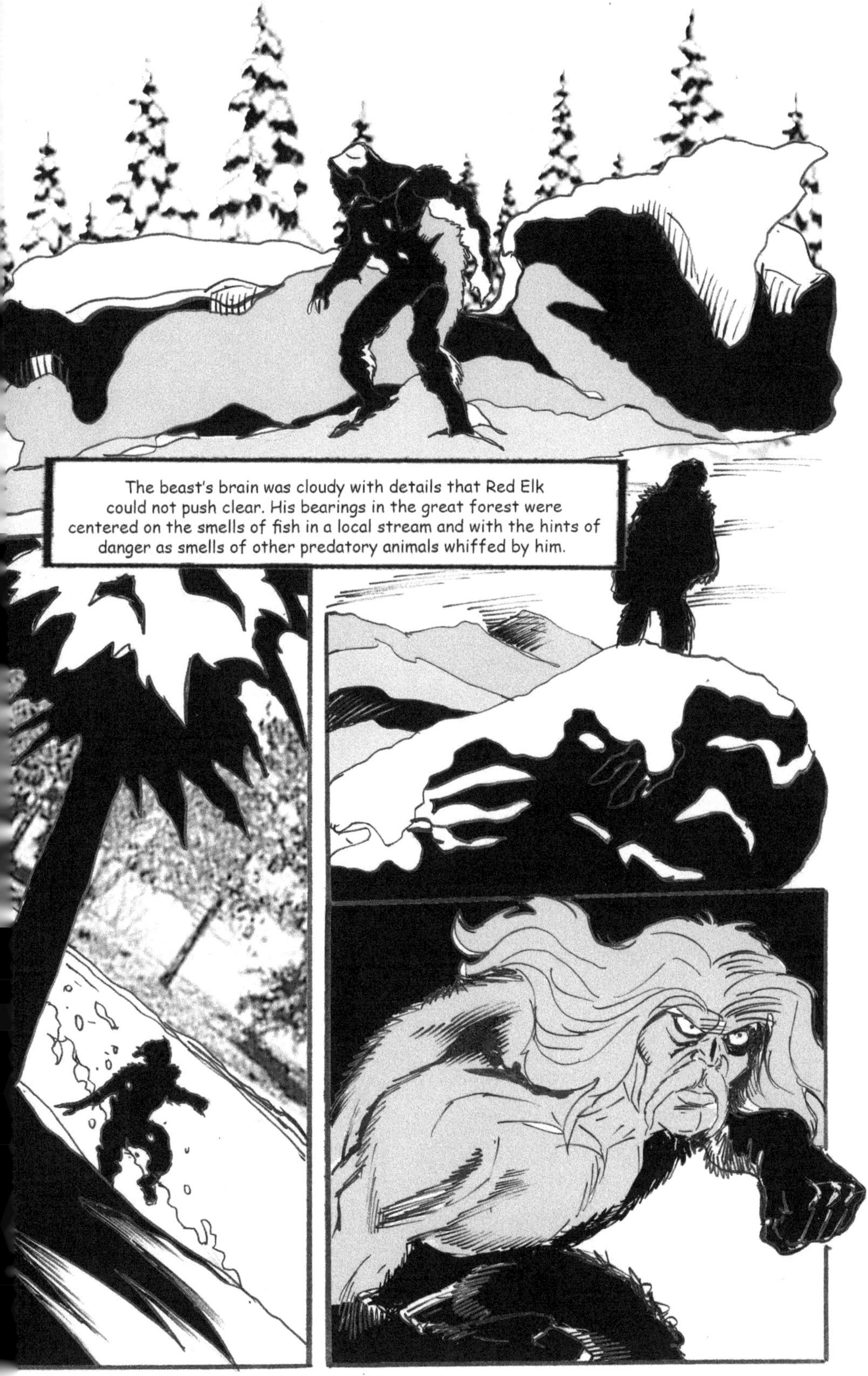
The beast's brain was cloudy with details that Red Elk could not push clear. His bearings in the great forest were centered on the smells of fish in a local stream and with the hints of danger as smells of other predatory animals whiffed by him.

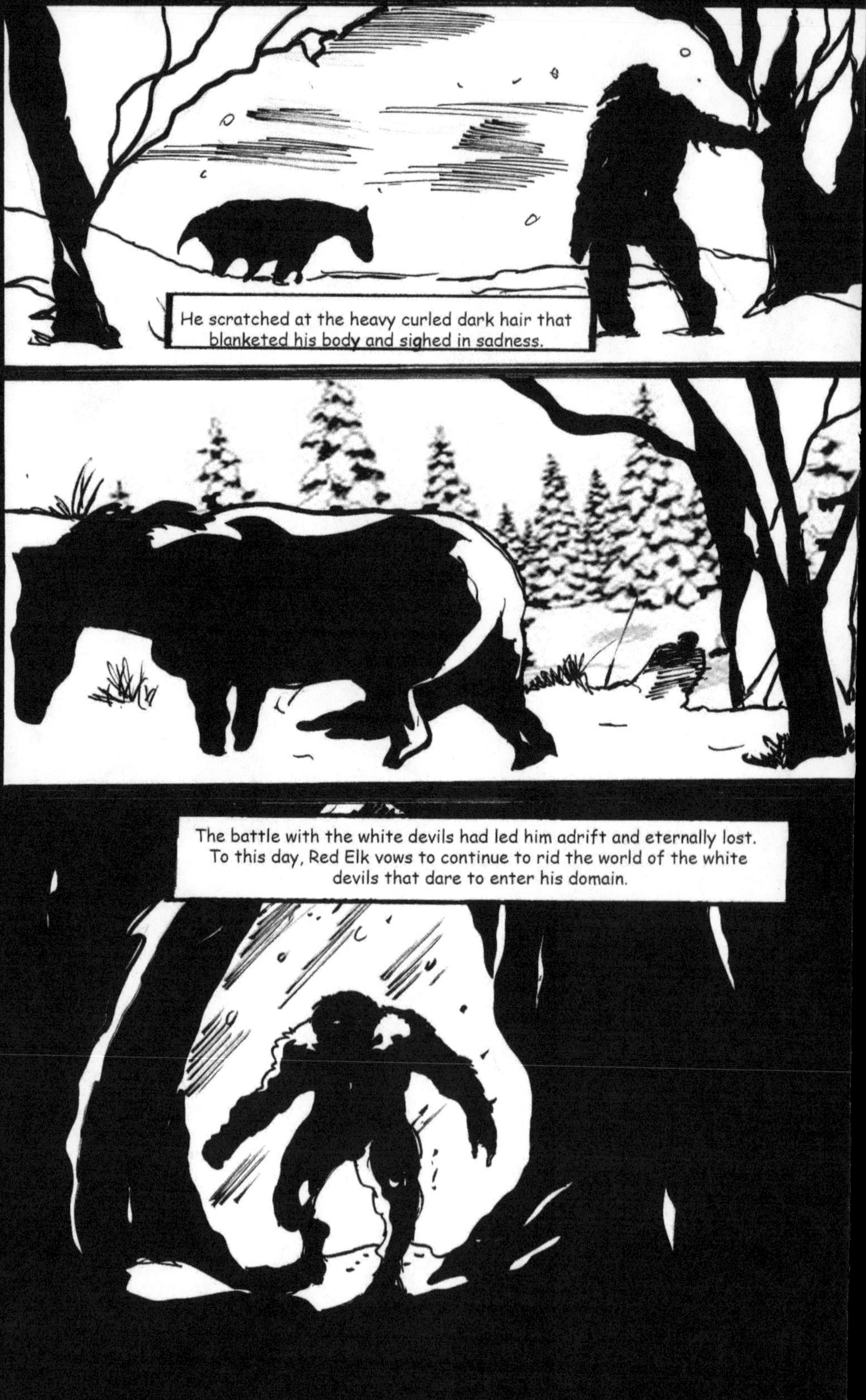
He scratched at the heavy curled dark hair that blanketed his body and sighed in sadness.
The battle with the white devils had led him adrift and eternally lost. To this day, Red Elk vows to continue to rid the world of the white devils that dare to enter his domain.

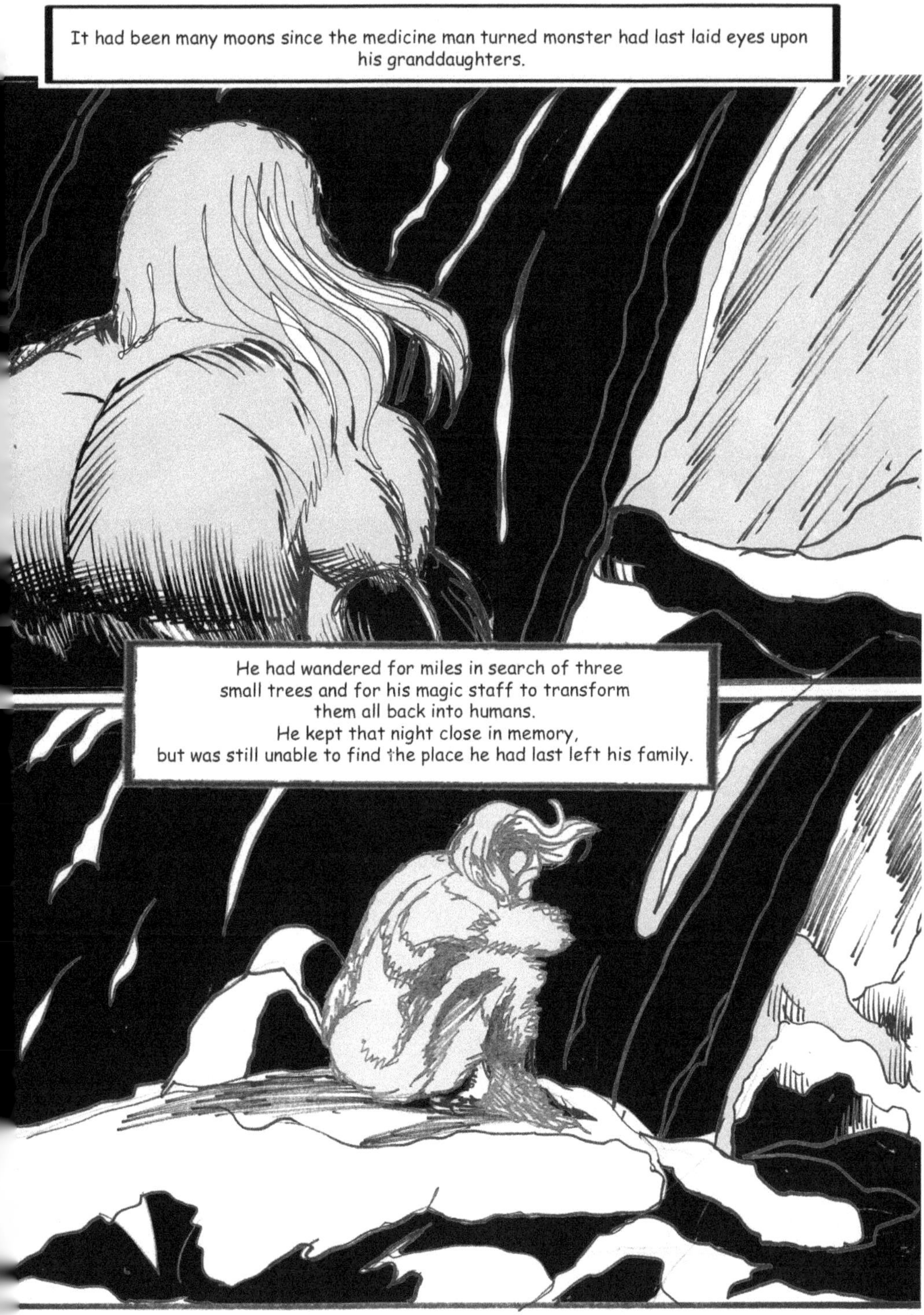
It had been many moons since the medicine man turned monster had last laid eyes upon his granddaughters.
He had wandered for miles in search of three small trees and for his magic staff to transform them all back into humans. He kept that night close in memory, but was still unable to find the place he had last left his family.

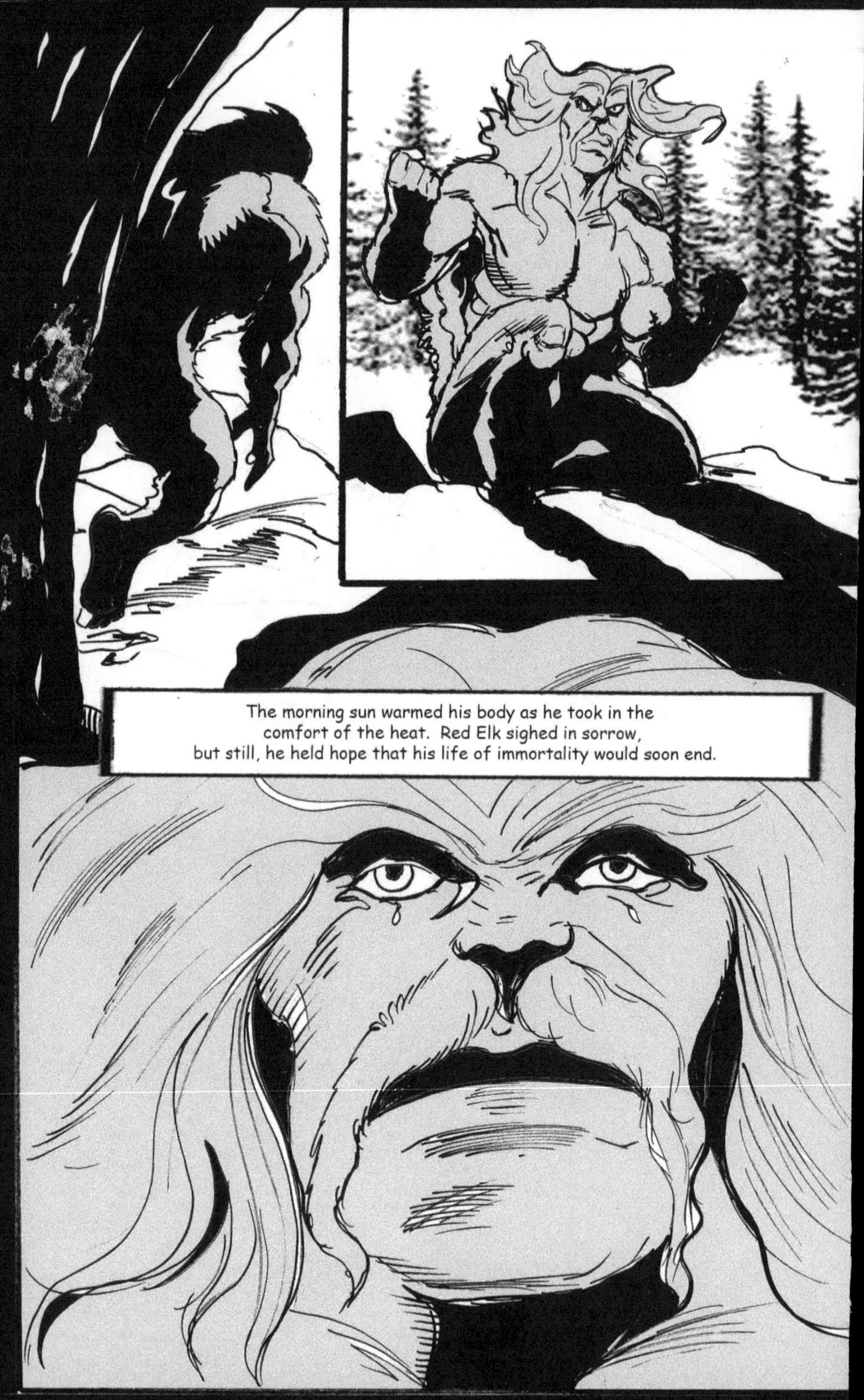
The morning sun warmed his body as he took in the
comfort of the heat. Red Elk sighed in sorrow,
but still, he held hope that his life of immortality would soon end.

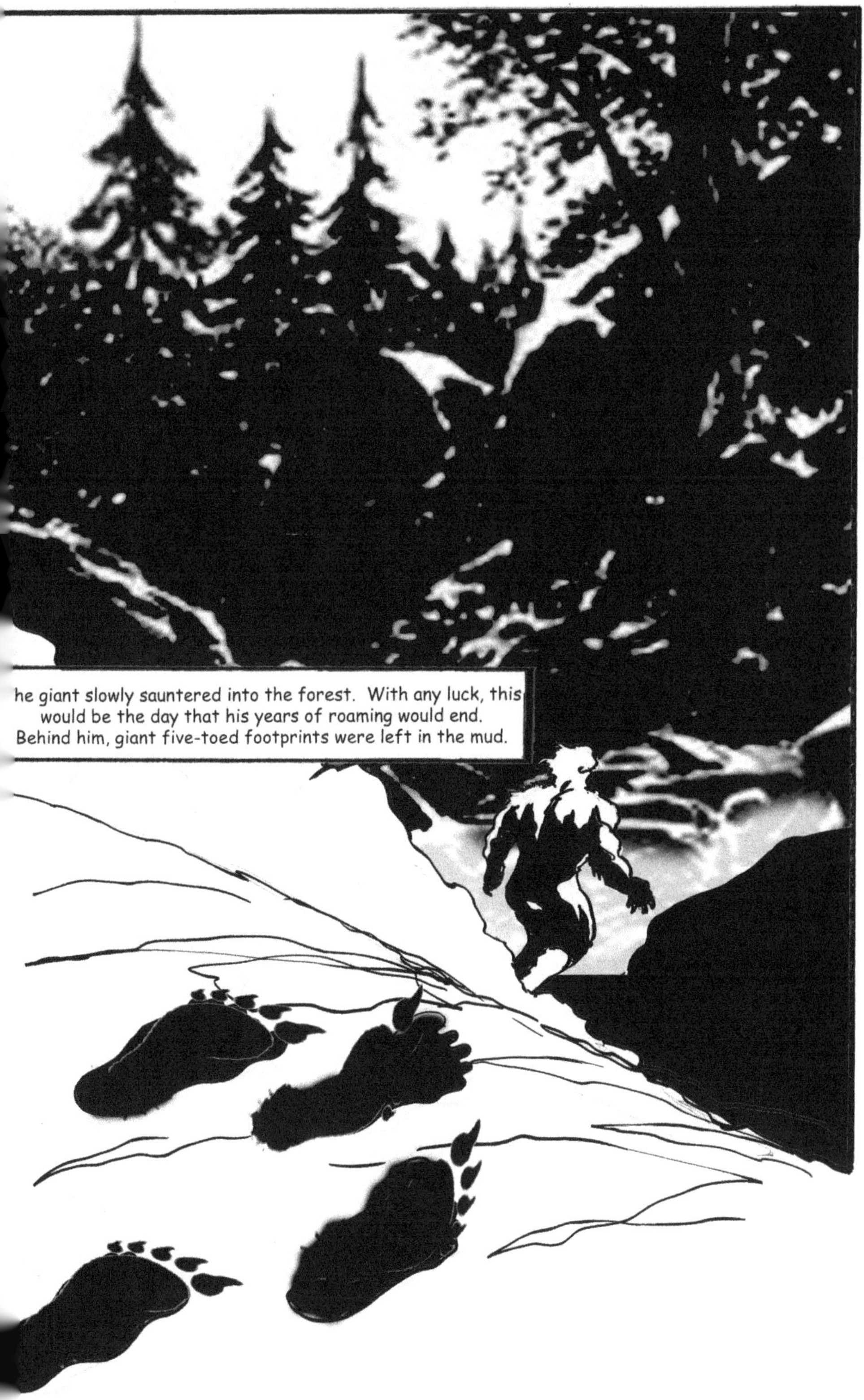
he giant slowly sauntered into the forest. With any luck, this
would be the day that his years of roaming would end.
Behind him, giant five-toed footprints were left in the mud.

CPSIA information can be obtained
at www.ICGtesting.com
Printed in the USA
JSHW051922150423
40238JS00020B/251